FIFTY PLACES TO FLY FISH

BEFORE YOU DIE

FIFTY PLACES TO
FLY FISH
BEFORE YOU DIE

Fly-Fishing Experts Share
the World's Greatest Destinations

Chris Santella

WITH SELECTED PHOTOGRAPHS BY
R. Valentine Atkinson

FOREWORD BY MIKE FITZGERALD, JR.
FRONTIERS INTERNATIONAL TRAVEL

STEWART, TABORI & CHANG · NEW YORK

For my parents, who encouraged me to follow my dreams,
and for my wife, Deidre, who continues to do so.

———

Published in 2004 by
Stewart, Tabori & Chang · 115 West 18th Street · New York, NY 10011
www.abramsbooks.com

Library of Congress Cataloging-in-Publication Data
Santella, Chris.
Fifty places to fly fish before you die : fly-fishing experts share the
world's greatest destinations / Chris Santella with selected photographs by
R. Valentine Atkinson ; foreword by Mike Fitzgerald, Jr.
p. cm.
ISBN 1-58479-356-2
1. Fly Fishing. I. Title.
SH456.S24 2004
799.12'4–dc22   2003070367

Printed in Thailand

10 9 8 7 6 5

Stewart, Tabori & Chang is a subsidiary of

LA MARTINIÈRE

Contents

ACKNOWLEDGMENTS

This book would not have been possible without the generous assistance of the expert anglers who shared their time and experience to help bring these fifty great fishing locales to life. To these men and women, I offer the most heartfelt thanks. I would especially like to thank Dan Callaghan, Nick Lyons, and Lefty Kreh, who offered encouragement and made many introductions on my behalf. I also wish to acknowledge the fine efforts of my agent, Stephanie Kip Rostan, my editor, Jennifer Lang, designer Paul Wagner, and copyeditor Don Kennison, who helped bring the book to fruition. I've had the good fortune over the last twenty-five years to make many fine fishing friends who have furthered my horizons, in terms of both angling experiences and a greater appreciation of life. This list includes Howard Kyser, Peter Marra, Ken Matsumoto, Jeff Sang, Joe Runyon, Mark Harrison, Peter Gyerko, Tim Purvis, Jack Ramsey, and Geoff Roach. I look forward to many more days on the river with these friends and friends to come. Finally, I want to extend a special thanks to my wife, Deidre, and my daughter, Cassidy, who've humored my absence on far too many occasions so I could pursue my favorite pastime.

FOREWORD

Someone once said that trout swim only in beautiful places. The same certainly holds for Atlantic salmon, steelhead, bonefish, and myriad other species fly fishermen pursue around the globe. What makes an angling destination great goes beyond the size of the fish or the numbers landed. Every fly-fishing expedition provides wonderful experiences. Prior to departure there is the excitement of the planning, the anticipation, and the accumulation of way more tackle and gear than any single person could possibly need.

A great fishing destination arouses all the senses. One celebrates the spectacular scenery, the local culture, the camaraderie among fishing friends, and the opportunity to spend time in the great outdoors. To me, the joy of fishing the world's great resources comes from the memories generated on each trip. It's spending time with close friends and meeting new ones. It's the epic battles and fish tales, many of which of course get exaggerated with time. It's having the opportunity to introduce your spouse or child to a river or destination you love. It's fishing with your father and grandfather, and cherishing those moments streamside for years to come. Such memories and great times induce me to keep my bags packed in anticipation of my next fly-fishing journey.

Chris Santella has compiled a list of some of the great fly-fishing locales this world has to offer in *Fifty Places to Fly Fish Before You Die*. He has consulted with many experts and seasoned professionals to provide accurate descriptions of each venue, while capturing the essence of each destination and the attributes that make every one special. I hope that you have the opportunity to fish some of the great waters he has featured. Each is remarkable in its own way.

There are many excellent fly-fishing opportunities for the intrepid traveling angler. In exchange for these lifetime experiences and memories, we have a responsibility to respect, protect, and, if necessary, restore these irreplaceable and invaluable fisheries so that they can be shared with future generations. Let this be your year to spend more time enjoying the great outdoors and to make the effort to introduce someone new to the wonderful sport of fly fishing.

MIKE FITZGERALD, JR.

FRONTIERS INTERNATIONAL TRAVEL

INTRODUCTION

My first fly-caught trout came to a Royal Coachman streamer fly that was sloppily cast and dragged across a stretch of the Saugatuck River just upstream of a parking lot in Westport, Connecticut. That stretch of river flowed through the middle of a corporate park. My catch was a rather sickly hatchery brown trout that was as foreign to its environs as was the angler on the other end of the line.

Needless to say, I was quite thrilled to have caught that trout. But having already feasted on back issues of *Fly Fisherman, Field & Stream,* and the like, I had more than a premonition that something better might be waiting: trout that had never seen the concrete walls of a hatchery; rivers that offered vistas beyond the receiving dock; a species of fish called steelhead; and other species I hadn't even read about yet.

I suppose this curiosity – this wanderlust to explore the many possibilities of the wide world of fly fishing – prompted me to begin thinking of some of the places I'd like to visit before my fishing days are finished. Thinking that there might be others out there with the same curiosity, I decided to write *Fifty Places to Fly Fish Before You Die.*

To compile the list of fifty places, I sought professional advice: I interviewed master fly fishers about some of their favorite fly-fishing experiences. These experts range from fishing writers and editors to fly-shop owners, outfitters, booking agents, and professional fly tiers. Some anglers are household names ... at least in fishing households. Others may one day be just as well known. Some spoke of waters close to their homes, waters they are closely associated with; others spoke of places they've visited only once but that made a profound impression. These folks are experienced, and they possess the perspective to evaluate truly wonderful fishing experiences. Each of my essays is based on one of their recommendations. To give a sense of the breadth of their angling experience, a short biography of each individual is included after each essay.

What criteria, you might ask, define a place to "fly fish before you die"? Is it a place where you can catch the most fish? The biggest fish? The smartest fish? The most exotic fish? Sometimes. And sometimes it's a place where the sun or moon happened to shine a certain way through the hills or palm trees, where a fish took a fly with a certain reckless abandon – or refused a fly with a resolve that bordered on arrogance. Or perhaps it's a place where the fish were completely uncooperative but the scenery was perfectly

OPPOSITE:
Bonefish and
giant trevally
await anglers
on the flats
of Christmas
Island.

transcendent. Like a timeless piece of art, a treasured fly-fishing experience often resists categorization, the essence of its greatness remaining open to interpretation.

While this book collects fifty memorable fishing experiences, it does not attempt to rank the waters discussed or the quality of the experiences these fisheries afford. One angler's nirvana might well be another's purgatory ... or worse. To dispel any notions of ranking, the fifty venues are listed alphabetically by locale.

In the hope that a few readers might decide to embark on adventures of their own, I have provided some "If You Go" information at the end of each section. It is by no means exhaustive but it will give would-be travelers a starting point for planning their trip. I've also included some tackle tips to give you a sense of what the local fly shops and outfitters recommend.

If you're planning a more complicated fishing adventure, especially to an exotic destination, I strongly advise working through a booking agent. A reputable agent can provide firsthand knowledge on what to expect and can help you navigate the plane tickets, transfers, visa requirements, equipment requirements, and other minutiae that can make the difference between a memorable trip and a tangled mess.

Reviewing the list of fifty places I've compiled with my expert assistants, I realize that to date I've been fortunate enough to fish nearly one-third of the venues. Not always well, and not always with "catching" success, but enough at least to get a taste of the experience they afford. As a forty-year-old male in relatively good health, the actuarial tables would indicate that I have decent odds to live at least another thirty-five years. That would mean that I need to knock off about one fishery a year to complete the list. It's hard work but someone has to do it!

I hope that this book helps you to launch a few adventures of your own.

Note: Every effort has been made to verify the accuracy of travel information at the time of publication. However, because price and outfitter programs are subject to change, we encourage you to research your adventure in greater detail before booking a trip.

OPPOSITE:
Hunting golden
dorado on
Estero Ibera in
Argentina.

THE DESTINATIONS

RAINBOW TROUT AND SILVER
SALMON AROUND BRISTOL BAY

RECOMMENDED BY **Leon Gorman**

The Bristol Bay area of Alaska, two hundred miles southwest of Anchorage, offers some of the greatest freshwater fishing diversity available anywhere. During the short Alaska summer, visitors can anticipate tussles with one or more species of Pacific salmon (what you'll catch depends on when you visit), rainbow trout, grayling, arctic char, resident and sea-run Dolly Vardens, pike, and lake trout. The fisheries vary from bigger rivers like the Togiak, Nushagak, and Wood, to lakes such as the Nuyukuk and Tikchik, to countless unnamed creeks. Three mountain ranges – the Kilbuck Mountains, the Taylor Mountains, and the Aleutian Range – and abundant wildlife (including brown bear, moose, and caribou) provide the classic Alaska backdrop that visitors anticipate.

OPPOSITE:
An angler
works a remote
stream in the
Bristol Bay
region of south-
west Alaska.

Leon Gorman timed his Bristol Bay adventure to coincide with the region's prolific runs of silver salmon. He came away more impressed with the big rainbows he encountered on a small tundra stream. "One day, we flew out to this little stream – in places it wasn't more than twelve feet wide. The stream was a long series of oxbows, about a mile in length. The strategy was simple. We'd kneel down to keep a low profile and cast downstream to where the oxbow looped. We were using huge Muddlers to simulate a dead mouse. The current would take the fly around the oxbow and out of sight. A second later the water would explode, and you'd have a big rainbow on. There was quite a ruckus in that little stream when the fish came on. The fish would be all over the place. In a couple of hours, I got three rainbows that exceeded ten pounds each. There was a lot of anticipation as the fly drifted around the corner. I had to remind myself to look over my shoulder now and again to keep a lookout for bears!"

Trophy rainbows are certainly a major attraction of the Bristol Bay region, and the Auglapak, Agulawok, and Alagnak are prime venues. In the early season, fish focus on

17

salmon smolt, augmenting their diet with the occasional mouse or vole as well as sporadic insect hatches (attractor patterns will generally suffice). When salmon begin returning and spawning ensues, the 'bows become more single-minded, gorging on eggs. After spawning is completed, they will dine on drifting salmon flesh, making flesh flies the preferred pattern. Not quite as elegant as dapping dainty duns, but a small compromise for some very big fish.

Variety is the spice of life during a stay at one of Bristol Bay's many lodges, and the fishing program is set up to accommodate a spectrum of experiences. Most fishing days begin with a brief jaunt in a floatplane and perhaps a jet-boat ride. Want to battle some very big fish? Visit in June, pop over to the Togiak or Rainbow River, and rig up your 10-weight with a high-density sink tip for chinook salmon that can reach 50 pounds. (Sometimes, floating line and an indicator will do the trick.) Want to switch gears completely? Grab a 4- or 5-weight and a handful of dry flies and head over to the Agulawok or Upper Nushagak for grayling, which are tremendous light-tackle sport. Feel like a break from salmonids? How about pike on Lake Beverly or Tikchik Lake? The northerns will eagerly take popping bugs and other flies stripped along the surface, and go to 15 pounds.

Thanks to the abundance of arctic char that gather at lake mouths to intercept salmon smolt making their way to the Pacific, you can catch your lunch and continue fishing until the char has been prepared to your liking.

While Bristol Bay's aggressive rainbows proved a greater challenge for Leon's group, the fast and furious silver fishing provided some memorable moments. "At one point, four of us were along a sandbar, casting over a school of incoming silvers. I was farthest downstream. As I followed my fly on its swing, I saw a fly line drifting by – a fish had separated the fly line from my friend's backing and was heading downstream. I grabbed the line with the fish still attached, and walked it up the bar to my friend. Together, we managed to get the line reattached to the backing. Eventually, he landed the fish."

No Bristol Bay angling adventure is quite complete without a bear story, and Leon's trip did not disappoint. "We were flying out to fish one day and came upon a grizzly. The pilot flew down for a closer look. The bear got up on his hind legs and shook his paws at us, as if he were ready for a fight. It was wonderful to see such a great animal. Though I have to say that I was glad we encountered him from the plane, rather than on that little tundra stream where we got the big rainbows."

LEON GORMAN, grandson of L. L. Bean, currently serves as chairman of the board of L. L. Bean, Inc. Leon and his wife, Lisa, have championed a number of conservation programs in Maine and nationally. Among these are the effort to preserve the St. John River in northern Maine; establishing a marine resource education center at Bowdoin College, his alma mater; and supporting the Appalachian Mountain Club. Under Leon's leadership, L. L. Bean has established itself as an environmentally responsible company whose support has included nearly $3 million in the past five years to conservation organizations. Leon has fished in Montana, New Brunswick, Labrador, Belize, and elsewhere but Maine fishing remains his favorite.

IF YOU GO

▶ **Prime Time:** The drainages of the Bristol Bay area are open from mid-May through the end of September. Freshwater species (rainbows, grayling, char, pike) are available throughout the year; silvers apprear in August and September.

▶ **Getting There:** You'll need to get to Dillingham, Alaska, where you'll be transferred to either a jet boat or floatplane to deliver you to your lodge. Commercial flights to Dillingham are available from Anchorage via Alaska Airlines.

▶ **Accommodations:** Some of Alaska's most storied lodges serve the Bristol Bay region. Two perennial favorites are Bristol Bay Lodge (509-964-2094; www.bristolbaylodge.com) and Tikchik Narrows Lodge (907-243-8450; www.tikchiklodge.com). Both lodges offer excellent food, nearby and fly-out fishing, and both carry a price tag of $6,200 for a week's visit, based on double occupancy. (Note that Bristol Bay Lodge guests spend two nights away from the main lodge at riverside outpost camps.)

▶ **Equipment:** A 9-foot 6- or 7-weight is preferred for rainbows. Most fishing is done with floating line, but bring a few sink-tips in case of high water. A standard assortment of dry-fly patterns will cover most hatches. An assortment of bead head nymphs, egg patterns, Muddler Minnows, Woolly Buggers, Egg-Sucking Leeches, flesh flies, and deer-hair mice will round out your offerings. Match a salmon rig to the fish that will be present; most anglers prefer a 9- or 10-weight for kings, an 8-weight for silvers and chum, and a 7-weight for sockeyes and pinks. Bring both floating and sink-tip lines; your guides will have favorite flies for each species.

SILVER SALMON ON NAKALILOK BAY

RECOMMENDED BY **Tammy Corb**

As someone who books lots of fly-fishing trips to Alaska, Tammy Corb has her finger on the trends – both good and bad. "One of the things I hear a lot from people is, 'I went all the way to Alaska, and found myself fishing among other people and other boats. I didn't expect that and I was a little disappointed.'" This is not likely to happen at Alaska Wilderness Safari's camp on Nakalilok Bay, which is situated on the Pacific side of the Alaska Peninsula. It's arguably the most isolated coastal fishing camp in Alaska, and one of the best places in the world to pursue chrome-bright, ocean-fresh silver salmon.

"'Isolated' is the word," Tammy said. "There's not another settlement up and down the coast for a hundred miles or more, and no roads for three hundred fifty miles. The camp has a concession to operate in the middle of the four-point-three-million-acre Alaska Wilderness Area. The odds are very high that you won't see another boat, another plane, or another human, except the people in your group."

The camp was established in 1984 by J. W. Smith, who already had a lodge on Bristol Bay at a place called Painter Creek. The Pacific side was the most remote area of Alaska, and J.W. was curious about what was over there. He loaded up a backpack and hiked over the Chiginigak Mountains. It was only forty or fifty miles, but it took a week, as there were no trails. He found an abundance of short-run streams, most fewer than twenty miles long. But there was enough rain to fill them, and incredible numbers of fish.

"When I was doing the exploratory trips, it wasn't easy going," J.W. said. "We didn't have Gore-Tex then, and we didn't have room to carry a tent or waders. I slept in a tarp, and we waded wet in our hiking boots. The one luxury I carried was butter, to keep the calories coming. A high-end meal was a fish wrapped in foil with a stick of butter. I like to joke that I'm the founding father of that section of Alaska."

OPPOSITE:
Visitors to
Nakalilok Bay
will find many
silver salmon,
some brown
bears, and no
other people.

21

The number of fish that congregate at Nakalilok Bay is astounding. "There's a fairly steep beach that pans down into the ocean," J. W. explained. "If the wind is offshore, you can wade out into the ocean and fish. On a calm day, the salmon will daisy-chain along the surf line, so it's only a forty-foot cast. There have been times when there are strings of fish three miles long. Sometimes you'll see their little faces in the waves. If the sun is out, you can discern the different salmon species."

Silver salmon or coho (*Oncorhynchus kisutch*) are sought by fly fishers more than the other five species of Pacific salmon because of their willingness to slam a fly – Woolly Buggers, Egg-Sucking Leeches, and a pink deer-hair monstrosity called a Pollywog. Fish fresh from the ocean show a great proclivity toward Pollywogs that are skated over them, and often cartwheel frantically when hooked. "If you're fishing a Pollywog, the fish will sometimes follow it on the surface for a while before taking the fly, making a wake," Tammy described. "I know it's cliché, but it reminds me of *Jaws*, especially with the males' hooked jaws." According to J.W., there are three conditions for success when fishing Pollywogs: "You have to have calm water. You have to have a lot of fish. And you want to have light skies, or even bright sun. If you have all these conditions working, you can do as well as swinging a wet fly."

The silvers of Nakalilok Bay are plentiful. They are also larger than the fish found on other Alaska drainages. The silvers returning to the Pacific side of the peninsula spend a bit more time at sea feeding before they arrive at their home stream. This brings their average weight up to 12 to 15 pounds. Fish in the high teens are pretty common.

"You don't have to go far from the camp to get to fishing," Tammy added. "There are three unnamed streams that actually run through the periphery of the camp – one's just a five-minute walk. You're fishing in fairly small water – knee to thigh high. You can watch the fish stacking up as the tide rises. Because the fish are right from the ocean, they're very strong. The fishing can be frantic. Some of the takes were so explosive, I thought they were going to take my arm off. It's eerie in a way, because it's so quiet. There's not even the sound of a generator in the background. When a fish takes, the silence is punctuated by the scream of the reel."

Anglers fishing near the mouth of the streams will occasionally have a bigger fish strip off a hundred yards of backing and return to the ocean. It's not uncommon to catch thirty to forty fish in a day, whether you're a beginner or an advanced fisherman. Fresh fish come in on every tide. You can actually target individual fish, if you so choose, which is not the norm for silvers. If anglers wish, they can stalk silvers on the flats of the bay as the tide comes in. It's rather like hunting very large bonefish in cold water amid volcanoes, glaciers, and brown bears. (If you wear yourself out on silvers, Dolly Varden and arctic char up to 8 pounds are also available.)

Anglers visiting Nakalilok Bay enjoy comfortable tent accommodations and other civilized amenities, though at the end of the day one must still be prepared to weather the elements. "You're on the northern Pacific," Tammy advised. "You get rain, fog, and wind when the fronts come through, which happens regularly. But on the other side of the coin, when you get clear weather the beauty simply takes your breath away."

And you never forget who really owns the land. Brown bears often feed in the bay in front of the camp. To maintain some order, J.W. keeps a bear perimeter, which works like the invisible fence that some dog owners use. When bears come into camp – and they usually do each week – J.W. is notified, so he can shoo them away. Nakalilok Bay is not for the faint of heart.

TAMMY CORB started at Frontiers International Travel at the tender age of sixteen, working as a part-time office assistant. After high school, she joined full time and hasn't looked back. Working at Frontiers opened up an incredible array of fishing opportunities, sending Tammy packing to New Zealand, Venezuela, the Kola Peninsula of Russia, British Columbia, and throughout the American West. She is currently Alaska Program Manager for Frontiers; her work has taken her to more than thirty fishing venues in the forty-ninth state.

IF YOU GO

▶ **Prime Time:** Mid-August through September.

▶ **Getting There:** Nakalilok Bay can be reached only by a forty-five-minute bush-plane flight from King Salmon, Alaska; flights leave Saturday mornings. Visitors will often overnight on Friday in Anchorage and take an early-morning jet flight to King Salmon. If the weather is clear, the flight to Nakalilok Bay can be awesome, with bears, moose, and caribou often observed. The bush plane times its departure to coincide with low tide, as it lands on a tidal flat adjacent to camp.

▶ **Accommodations:** Alaska Wilderness Safaris (800-211-4753; www.rodgunresources.

com) hosts the one and only camp on Nakalilok Bay. Because the camp rests on a wilderness preserve, it must be broken down at the end of each season. Despite this, the accommodations are quite comfortable, including hot showers and first-rate camp meals. The cost is $4,300 per person per week (based on double occupancy), and includes guides, meals, cocktails, and two helicopter fly-out days to rivers that are even more remote. (Price does not include charter flight from and to King Salmon, which is approximately $350.)

▶ **Equipment:** A 9-foot 8- or 9-weight rod fitted with floating line and 200 yards of backing will satisfy your silver needs; if you also want to fish for Dollys and char, bring a 5- or 6-weight outfit. Silvers aren't leader shy; 9-foot leaders tapered to 0x and tippet from 10 to 25 pounds will suffice. Basic Alaska flies (Egg-Sucking Leeches, Crystal Buggers, egg patterns, etc.) in #2–8 will do for subsurface fishing; for heart-stopping surface takes, bring pink Deer Hair or Foam Pollywogs in #2.

LANDLOCKED SALMON
ON RIO TRAFÚL

RECOMMENDED BY **Ernest Schwiebert**

Ernest Schwiebert first traveled to Patagonia at a time when Argentina was better known for its beef than for its wine and trout. *Life* magazine had published an extensive photo essay on fly fishing that featured Ernie, along with Roderick Haig-Brown and several other anglers. Soon after, *Sports Illustrated* decided to do a fishing story of its own, and approached Ernie to do the piece, as *Life* had made him somewhat famous. "The editors at *Sports Illustrated* asked, 'If we were to send you to an exotic location to do a trout-fishing story, where should it be?' I gave it a moment's thought and said, 'Patagonia.'" Ernie spent ten weeks in the Argentine in 1959 and 1960, and he was able to see the country from Rio Pico to Zapala. "It was remarkable," Ernie recalled, "like Wyoming when the only scars across the frontier were the ruts of the Oregon Trail." There were very few fishing guides in Argentina at that time, and no outfitters or fishing lodges. However, some of the local people were quite generous with their knowledge, and Ernie found plenty of big fish.

Ernie has been back to Argentina more than thirty times since, and a river that remains a favorite is the Rio Trafúl. The fifteen miles of Rio Trafúl are bordered on the north by Estancia Arroyo Verde, a ranch that has hosted anglers – including presidents and potentates – for more than seven decades. (The land on the south side of the river was once the family's Estancia La Primavera, which was fished by President Dwight Eisenhower and was recently bought by Ted Turner, who's been known to have a keen eye for good fishing habitat.) Many anglers who know rank Arroyo Verde among the best fishing destinations in the world for the splendor of its Andean setting, the grace and sophistication of its hosts, Maurice and Mercedes Lariviere, and the quality of the fly fishing on the Rio Trafúl.

Rio Traful runs crystalline and limpid from a large, fjord-size lake called Lago Traful. It is home to large rainbow and brown trout and – an added bonus – landlocked Atlantic salmon, introduced almost a century ago from Lake Sebago in Maine. Anglers here quest for quality, not quantity. During most weeks of the season, anglers will have shots at fish in the 5- to 10-pound class. Rainbows and landlocks eclipsing 20 pounds have been landed, brook trout at 10 pounds are possible, and the Rio Traful's current record brown weighed in at 16 pounds. There can be good fly hatches at times, though visiting anglers cannot count on them. The bigger fish feed heavily on baitfish and unique Andean crayfish that resemble small saltwater crabs. Sight-fishing with small nymphs and large blue-and-white baitfish imitations can be very productive when conditions are right.

The beauty of the surroundings cannot be overstated. Several great batholiths of rhyolite rise from the river to heights of two thousand feet and more; there are condor rookeries here. Other parts of the valley are studded with grayish-amber sandstone formations, reminiscent of Yosemite and the Dolomite Alps of northern Italy. "I've often teased the Larivieres that they own a private national park," Ernie recalled. "They not only own the whole valley and its famous river, but they also own the mountains ... and the far side of some mountains. I often walked out on the lawn in the morning and evening light and tried to imagine how it might feel to own the Traful."

Back in 1992, *Fly Fisherman* editor John Randolph visited the Traful with an outfitter from Bariloche and reported the presence of an unusually large fish in a pool cut by a recent winter flood – at that time, the pool was still without a name. Randolph and his guide mistook the fish for a mammoth brown when, in fact, it was a landlocked Atlantic salmon that had returned to the river from the lake before spawning in May. Every serious angler in the province had heard about the great fish, which was estimated to be as large as 30 pounds.

When Ernie visited Arroyo Verde that year, he was badgered into trying his luck. "We studied its behavior from the cliffs for a time," Ernie said. "The fish kept opening and closing its mouth, and some thought it was feeding. I believe its head and jaws were changing shape as part of the male's pre-spawning process, and that we'd have to tease it into striking. I'd be forced to stalk on hands and knees to avoid spooking it, and use a big smelt pattern along the lines of a size 2/0 Blue and White Deceiver." Ernie worked on the fish all morning and into the afternoon, casting the fly above its station and stripping it back, getting closer and closer. Eventually, such tactics aroused the salmon's interest. "The fish was chasing the fly and even exploded into the shallows at one point, until its belly was rubbing on the rocks," Ernie recalled. "One time he got so close he splashed me with water as he turned away and bolted."

Meanwhile, back at the big house, a formal luncheon was being planned, with guests that included a former Argentine ambassador to the United Kingdom. Ernie had been given a command invitation to attend lunch on time. "I didn't have a watch," Ernie continued. "I was afraid that a flash of light off its case might spook the fish. Watching it chase my fly got so exciting that I forgot the time. I finally yelled out to the guides on the bluff, who were spotting the fish for me and describing its reactions to our tactics, 'What time is it?' They yelled 'three o'clock.' I thought, 'We're dead meat!'"

When they returned to the ranch, Mémé Lariviere was glaring at them from the dining salon and Maurice was shaking his head. "I apologized," Ernie said, "and told them how we had nearly got the fish. I added that if it stayed in its current aggressive mood, we'd have another chance to get him. I went to wash up and returned to the dining room. I could see that my table setting and crystal had been removed. Mémé intercepted me before I entered and muttered brusquely, 'Malcriados' – which can mean anything from naughty children to badly bred ruffians, depending on one's expression and tone of voice." Her eyes were laughing, but her tone was stern.

Everyone was eager to hear about the fish, and any bad feelings were soon forgotten. After lunch, Ernie and the young guides returned to the river. As the twilight gathered, the fish dropped into the tail shallows of the pool. Ernie was finally able to get the big salmon to chase the fly again; it made several immense, splashy rolls. "As it was getting dark, I finally saw the fish take the fly," Ernie said. "It jumped twice, resembling a pig trying to fly, but it fell back clumsily, like a box kite with too much tail." Fortunately, the fish bolted upstream into the deepest section of the pool; fast water and the cliffs two hundred yards downstream would have precluded chasing it. Ernie finally tailed the fish, a 37.5-inch male that was estimated at 22 to 24 pounds, the biggest salmon the Larivieres had ever seen taken with a fly on the Rio Traful. "I was overjoyed to see that the ancestral Sebago Lake genes from 1904 were alive and well," Ernie said. "And we happily released it." The same fish was spotted by the ranch foreman later that year on the spawning redds.

When Ernie reached the house everyone was excited, and on the last morning of his visit he was asked to enter the fish into the fishing log. "I asked, 'What shall we call the pool?'" Ernie reminisced. "The Larivieres responded, 'We simply call it the New Pool.' Several other names were quickly suggested and dropped. 'Ernie's Pool?' I said 'No!' 'What about Schwiebert's Pool?' I said 'No! Such a pool deserves an honest Spanish name.' As the debate among the anglers and guides continued, Mémé entered the room and said quietly, 'The pool already has a name – I've decided to call it Los Malcriados.'"

ERNEST SCHWIEBERT is an award-winning architect and perhaps the most celebrated angling writer of our time. His fishing books include *Matching the Hatch*, *Salmon of the World*, *Death of a Riverkeeper*, *A River for Christmas*, *The Compleat Schwiebert*, *The Traveling Angler*, *The Henryville Flyfishers*, and the boxed two-volume *Trout*. Ernest has also served as a contributing editor for *Sports Afield* and was founding editor at large for *Fly Fisherman*, and he has written for scores of magazines, including *Field & Stream*, *Outdoor Life*, *Life*, *Esquire*, *Sports Illustrated*, the *New York Times*, and the *Atlantic Monthly*. His fishing books have been awarded the Arnold Gingrich Literary Prize from the Theodore Gordon Flyfishers, the Charles Kunkel Fox Literary Award from Trout Unlimited, and the Aldo Starker Leopold Award from the National Park Service. His fly-fishing honors include conservation awards from Trout Unlimited, the Theodore Gordon Flyfishers, and the Federation of Fly Fishers.

IF YOU GO

▶ **Prime Time:** If you hope to tangle with Rio Traful's landlocked salmon, the best time to be there is from the middle of March to the middle of May.

▶ **Getting There:** You'll first fly to Buenos Aires and then on to either Bariloche or San Martin. Both towns are served by Aerolineas Agentinas.

▶**Accommodations:** Your home for fishing Rio Traful will be Arroyo Verde, where the Larivieres accommodate anglers with lavish afternoon dinners and late suppers. All-inclusive rates are $600 per day per person based on double occupancy.

▶ **Equipment:** For the beginning of the season, a 9-foot 7- or 8-weight rod is best; from the middle of January onward, 5- or 6-weights are advisable. Bring floating, sink-tip, and fast-sinking lines. For sinking lines, short leaders in 12-pound test will suffice; 12- or 14-foot leaders are best for floating lines, tapered from 4x to 0x. Standard streamers work well. Adams, Royal Wulff, and Humpies (in #6 to #16) cover many Traful hatches.

GOLDEN DORADO ON ESTERO IBERA

RECOMMENDED BY **Craig Derby**

Mention fly fishing and Argentina in the same breath, and most anglers think of the mountainous region of Patagonia and its wonderful trout. Something far different awaits you in the subtropical marshlands of Estero Ibera in northeastern Argentina: the golden dorado. Golden dorado (*Salminus maxillosus*) were largely unknown outside of Argentina a decade ago, but their bellicose temperament, epic strength, and otherworldly beauty have catapulted them onto many anglers' "must fish for" lists. Goldens have the shape of a salmon, the jaws of a crocodile, and scales of yellow, orange, and black that radiate the fish's namesake golden sheen. Called the "tiger of the river" by some and a freshwater bonefish by others, golden dorado are not at all related to the saltwater species of dorado, sometimes called dolphin. In fact, biological studies suggest that dorado are a unique species, perhaps a turbocharged relative of the minnow. Their range includes southern Brazil, parts of Bolivia, Paraguay, and Uruguay and on down through northeastern Argentina to the mouth of the Paraná River at Buenos Aires. There are tales of goldens reaching weights of close to 100 pounds in some of the bigger rivers, though in Estero Ibera most fish encountered are between 4 and 15 pounds. This is more than enough fish for fly rodders. The biggest fish landed on a fly thus far was 25 pounds.

Craig Derby first learned about golden dorado from a fishing buddy. "A friend of mine had read about goldens years ago as a child," Craig recalled. "He'd always wanted to catch one, and asked me if I'd be interested in joining him. I started researching it myself, and three years ago we went down to Estero Ibera." On his first visit, Craig had some very good fishing, including a fish of 13 pounds. The marshes were equally impressive. Estero Ibera comprises 3.5 million acres of undeveloped creeks, channels, lagoons, swamps, and lakes. Rio Corrientes, a major tributary of the Paraná River, flows out of Estero Ibera

29

and holds many dorado. This remarkable ecosystem sustains a plethora of wildlife, including 350 bird species, freshwater stingrays, and a sizable population of American caiman – a large but harmless member of the crocodile family. Considering its subtropic environs, the waters of Estero Ibera stay surprisingly clear and cool; the marshlands act as a natural biofilter. The relative clarity of Estero Ibera makes fly rodding for goldens a worthwhile and inviting experience.

Fishing methods on the marshes are largely dependent on water levels. If the water is high, anglers can expect to do a good deal of blind-casting to likely looking lies against grass tussocks or the banks, with sinking lines and large streamers. "You'll pound the banks pretty hard," Craig said. "It's not dissimilar to bass fishing." When water levels are lower, and on many days near dusk, you can switch over to floating lines and even fish poppers. Under these circumstances, anglers can fish to sighted goldens. "There often is a magic half hour when the fish come up on the surface," Craig added. "It's quite a thing to see, especially with the backdrop of the fiery sunsets that you witness at Estero Ibera." Whether you hook them on the surface or on a sinking fly, the take and initial runs of the golden dorado are quite memorable. "They really hammer the fly," Craig said, "and they don't leave anything on the table. They fight like a last-round welterweight who's behind on the scorecard. Water is flying everywhere, their gills are flapping. They're not a stamina fish, but they are a photographer's dream, as they come out of the water so much in that first fit of fury." When you do get a fish to the boat, a boga grip and a dose of caution are recommended; goldens have some impressive choppers.

Whether fishing subsurface or surface, fast retrieves and strip-sets (as practiced in tarpon fishing) are mandatory. Many fine fish are lost by newcomers conditioned to lifting their rod tip to set the hook. At Pira Lodge, anglers attempt to make the most of lower-light hours; fishing is better then, and it allows you to beat the heat of the marsh. The regimen is to get on the water early, fish the morning, have a leisurely lunch and siesta midday, and then hit the water again by midafternoon and fish until dusk.

Golden dorado are an amazing sport fish and sure to excite anglers for years to come, though much of the joy of this adventure lies in the gestalt of this exotic and isolated land. "A trip to Ibera is as much an eco tour as a fishing experience," Craig said. "There are capybaras [the world's largest rodent] on the banks, swimming and foraging on weeds. Caimans are floating in the channels or lying on the banks. Screamers, gooselike birds with a raucous call, are everywhere. When they take off, they sound like a slow-

OPPOSITE:
Exotic in
appearance and
hard fighting,
golden dorado
have become
a much-sought-
after species.

bladed helicopter." At Pira Lodge, fine Euro-Argentine cuisine and the warm hospitality of the hosts round out the experience. By several reports, the recently constructed Pira Lodge may emerge as one of the finest fishing lodges anywhere. "The aesthetics of the place are extremely pleasing," Craig recalled. "And the staff is very enthusiastic about everything they do, both the food and the fishing."

CRAIG DERBY's initial love of fly fishing began when wet-wading the streams of northern California twenty-five years ago. Wanderlust and a love of exotic fisheries have taken him all over the world since. A practicing anesthesiologist, he currently spends as much time chasing fish and doing volunteer medical work abroad as he does working in his hometown of Bellingham, Washington. Recently, he has combined his lifelong love of photography with his fishing obsession to start Derby Digital Images.

IF YOU GO

▶ **Prime Time:** January through April provides the best fishing. The season is open September through May.

▶ **Getting There:** Estero Ibera is located four hundred miles due north of Buenos Aires. The Pira Lodge in Corrientes has a private landing strip, and flights can be charted from Buenos Aires. The journey can also be made by car; it's a seven-hour drive.

▶ **Accommodations:** Pira Lodge (www.piralodge.com) is on the coast of the Ibera marshlands near Rio Corrientes and caters to fly fishers. Lodging is luxurious by most standards, with air-conditioned rooms and private bathrooms. All-inclusive weeklong packages (lodging/meals/guides) range from $3,750 during peak season to $2,820 in nonpeak times. Space is limited to ten anglers per week.

▶ **Equipment:** A 9-foot 7- or 8-weight rod is adequate for golden dorado. You should bring three lines: a floating line (formulated for tropical conditions), plus a couple of fast-sinking lines like Teeny T-200 and T-300. Each line should have at least 100 yards of backing. For floating line, have 9-foot leaders in 0x, with 16-pound shock tippet and a wire leader; sinking lines require shorter leaders with shock tippet and wire leader. Lefty's Deceivers in a variety of colors in #1/0 to #4/0 are good producers. Cockroaches and Clouser Minnows are also effective. Poppers and divers in black, purple, chartreuse, white, and yellow can work well too, especially when the fish are aggressively feeding.

SEA-RUN BROWN TROUT ON
THE RIO GRANDE

RECOMMENDED BY **R. Valentine Atkinson**

Tierra del Fuego translates from the Spanish as "land of fire," and for fly anglers that fire springs from the sparks generated from backing that's ripped off the reel by the gargantuan sea-run brown trout of the Rio Grande.

Sea-run browns hold a special allure for anglers, for both their scarcity and their size. In a handful of rivers in northern Europe and South America, the fish can reach upward of 30 pounds. When they reach trophy size – say over 15 pounds – the sea-run browns begin to resemble Atlantic salmon; in fact, they are genetically related to *Salmo salar*. For photographer Val Atkinson, it is the sea-run's beauty as much as its challenge that makes it a special quarry. "Browns are my favorite trout," said Val. "They are splendidly colored, wary, and smart, which makes them a challenge. Sea-run browns are regular browns on steroids. The Rio Grande's healthy runs of fish make it arguably the finest sea-run-brown fishery in the world. When you feel the jolt of the sea-run's strike, and the head-shaking throb of a powerful fish that's on, your blood pressure is guaranteed to red-line."

The fishing possibilities of the Rio Grande and Tierra del Fuego were discovered in the late fifties by a handful of Argentine anglers and famed American fly fishers Joe Brooks and A. J. McClane. The windblown pampas country of southernmost South America, where condors with nine-foot wingspans patrol the skies and clean fallen sheep of their flesh in a flash, makes for an austere, otherworldly setting in the quest for an uncommon game fish. Today, three lodges provide guided access to some sixty miles of private river. The fish are plentiful enough to assure the competent angler scores of hook-ups in the course of a week, with fish averaging 8 to 10 pounds and the lunker 20-pound-plus fish always a possibility.

The technique for taking sea-run browns on the Rio Grande bears some similarity to

those used for two other anadromous species – steelhead and Atlantic salmon. Anglers cast across the current aiming for the far bank and the deeper water, using sink-tip or sinking lines to submerge the fly as deeply as possible before the swing begins; takes usually come on the swing. It is not terrifically technical fishing and the wading is generally easy, though the fierce gales that can scream off the Strait of Magellan can make even short casts a challenge. (Some of the wind-cheating lines on the market today can help you beat the breeze.) Large, dark streamers have comprised the traditional fly fare for Rio Grande sea-runs, though in low-water conditions smaller wets and even nymphs will sometimes outperform the proverbial Woolly Bugger.

As in the pursuit of most sea-run species, tenacity, rather than exactitude, will generally pay the biggest dividends, as this tale attests. Val and his companions had fished through the day, enjoyed a streamside dinner, and landed some good fish, ranging from 8 to 14 pounds. It was approaching eleven P.M., and Val reeled in his line and walked up to the top of the run where his fellow anglers were still casting away. "I could barely make out their shapes in the dark," Val recalled. "I thought I might as well make a few more casts myself. Running my hand along my leader, I noticed that I had a wind knot a few inches up from my number six Woolly Bugger. I decided to retie, as you never know." Tying a new knot was a challenge in the complete blackness, but Val managed, and then he returned to his spot downstream. On the very first cast, a powerful fish took the bugger. "I had strong tippet on," Val continued, "so I wasn't particularly worried ... at first. Then the fish started running downstream and into my backing. Browns aren't particularly known for their blinding long runs, but this guy was doing a job on me.

"Eventually, the other guys showed up, and I let them know I had a good fish on. After watching me for a while, they said, 'Sure Val, hurry up and bring him in so we can get back to the lodge' – thinking it was another eight-pounder. I finally got him up on the gravel and our guide shined his flashlight down into the whiskey-colored water. All conversation stopped as we stared down into the eyes of a monster. I tried to pick up the fish but was shaking so bad from the cold and the excitement that I couldn't do it. So we weighed the fish in the net. It was twenty-three pounds and three ounces – what turned out to be the second-largest fish caught on the Rio Grande that year."

R. VALENTINE ATKINSON is an internationally acclaimed photographer specializing in fly-fishing lifestyle and nature worldwide. His assignments have taken him to twenty-

OPPOSITE:
Tierra del Fuego
provides a stark
backdrop for
battling giant
sea-run browns.

seven countries. He divides his work between advertising and corporate and editorial photography, and is regularly published in most major fishing magazines. He has been the staff photographer for Frontiers International Travel for fifteen years and operates his own stock-photo library. Val has published two books, *Distant Waters* and *Trout & Salmon*. He was inducted into the Federation of Fly Fishers' Hall of Fame in 2003.

IF YOU GO

▶ **Prime Time:** The high season for sea-run browns on the Rio Grande is from Christmas through March, though fish are taken in November and April as well.

▶ **Getting There:** Tierra del Fuego is quite literally at the end of the world. To reach the Rio Grande, anglers must first fly to Buenos Aires, and then take another 1,800-mile flight to the town of Rio Grande in Tierra del Fuego. (Most visitors opt to overnight in Buenos Aires.)

▶ **Accommodations:** Similarities between the quest for sea-run browns and Atlantic salmon extend to the bill of fare. There is no public fishing access to the Rio Grande, and no place to escape the winds beside the lodges that cater to fly anglers. You'll pay a noble sum to fish the Rio Grande, up to $7,000 and more for a week's stay. But the good news is that, despite its far-flung location, Tierra del Fuego's lodges – Kua Tapen, Toon-Ken, and Estancia Maria Behety – are ranked among the finest in the world, providing first-rate guides, service, and cuisine. Openings are limited; if you can get a spot on the roster, your party will not see many other anglers.

▶ **Equipment:** A 9-foot 8-weight rod is the most popular weapon for the Rio Grande. Lighter spey rods (in 8- or 9-weight, 13 to 14 feet in length) are also becoming popular. Pack a floating line for low water and low-light conditions; a full sinking line (like a Teeny T-200) for deeper runs; and an intermediate sink-tip. A 9-foot tapered leader in 0x will do for floating lines; a few feet of mono in 8-, 10-, 12-, and 15-pound test will suffice for sinking lines. Popular flies include: Woolly Buggers in black and olive (#2-#6); Zonkers in dark colors (#2-#4); Peacocks (#2-#4); Girdle Bugs (#4-#12); and Collie Dog tube flies with aluminum or copper bodies.

BLACK MARLIN OFF CAIRNS

RECOMMENDED BY **Billy Pate**

Almost every sport has its frontier, its threshold, its Everest. For fly fishers, the Everest was billfish. How could you get them in casting range? How could you get them to take a fly? And how could you land a hundred-pound-plus fish on the high seas with a willowy – at least by blue-water standards – piece of fiberglass in your hand? Billy Pate was the man to climb that mountain. Since landing his first fly-caught billfish, he has gone on to catch all six billfish species on the fly, and holds ten world records for these conquests.

"I first went to Cairns in 1972, and caught the first black marlin on a fly. At the time, some people had talked about trying to catch billfish on flies, but only a few had done much about it. A guy who had been there recommended that I visit. He said there were a large number of juvenile fish around. It was funny. When we were around the docks, I thought that all the guys who go after the thousand-pounders – the 'granders,' as they call them – would look down on us with our little fly rods, going after the smaller fish. Instead, they were impressed. Eventually, the anglers there started a black marlin fly-fishing tournament."

Black marlin (*Makaira indica*) offer anglers about as much excitement as they can hope to handle on a fly rod. The fish are distributed throughout the tropical and sub-tropical waters of the Indian and Pacific oceans. Adult fish feed on squid, scad, king mackerel, frigate mackerel, dorado, and tuna, and can ultimately reach lengths of 15 feet and weights of 1,200 pounds and more. Unlike some species of billfish, black marlin sometimes favor shallower water and can be found within several miles of land. With backs of steel blue, black, and purple and stomachs of mauve and white, they are something to behold.

It is the juvenile fish, ranging anywhere from 30 to 150 pounds, that most fly anglers focus on at Cairns. The town sits on the northeast coast of Australia, opposite the Great Barrier Reef. Each September, the young fish gather inside the reef between Cairns and Cape Bowling Green near the city of Townsville. For many, this annual congregation offers the best opportunity in the world for an angler to land a marlin on a fly. Guides in Oz claim that some days the fish are so thick that anglers can have twenty shots at marlin in one day! Many world records have come from these rich waters, and it's quite likely that those records eventually will be shattered by fish caught there.

The "bait and switch" technique for attracting and hooking black marlin – or, for that matter, any billfish on a fly – is rather complex and demands some exceptional teamwork between the captain, his crew, and the angler. Once the fishing grounds are reached, a dead teaser fish on a bait rod is trolled behind the boat at slow speeds until it attracts the attention of a fish. The bait fish does not have hooks. When the marlin rises to the bait, one of the crew members reels in the teaser to draw the fish closer to the boat. Of course, it's essential to keep the teaser *just* out of reach of the fish. At this point, the fly angler steps into position and trails some line in the water, prepared to make what might very well be the cast of his or her life. When the fish is in fly-casting range (generally within thirty feet), the captain puts the boat in neutral, the angler presents a big honking fly a few feet to one side of the fish, and the teaser is hauled into the boat. Casts of twenty feet are often enough; the fish don't spook easily when they're chasing a meal. The marlin, it seems, is as excited by the teasing process as the angler, and the colors along its flanks radiate as it pursues the bait. When the fish takes, it will leap. Angling writer Jake Jordan has described the marlin's crash back to the ocean as "leaving a hole in the water that looks like a Volkswagen bus just fell from the sky." The battle that follows can last as long as several hours, and may forever change the way you think about fly fishing.

With the proximity of the Great Barrier Reef and a pleasant tropical climate, Cairns has become a popular tourist destination, even for those not seeking a billfish on a fly. The 1,250-mile coral reef is considered one of the best diving venues in the world, and the tropics of Queensland are home to unique rain forests. A number of other saltwater species are available for fly rodders. Close to shore, you'll find barramundi and giant trevally. In the blue water, you could encounter king mackerel, cobia, yellowfin tuna, bluefin tuna, and false albacore. And if the *smaller* black marlin are not enough for you, you can try your hand at the big fellows that show up outside the reef later in the fall.

BILLY PATE is considered the world's foremost big-game saltwater fly fisherman. He helped pioneer billfish fly-fishing techniques and was the first fly angler to catch all six species of billfish on a fly rod; he holds twenty-five fly-rod world records. A great tarpon aficionado, Billy estimates that he's jumped five thousand tarpon and one thousand bill-fish on a fly. Billy cofounded one of the first adventure angling companies, Worldwide Sportsman, and has fished in forty countries. He also helped design the popular fly reel that bears his name. In 2003, Billy was inducted into the International Game Fish Association (IGFA) Hall of Fame. Newcomers to billfish on a fly might do well to view Billy Pate's video, *Fly Fishing for Billfish*.

IF YOU GO

▶ **Prime Time:** September is the time that juvenile black marlin are inside the Great Barrier Reef in greatest numbers, though some fish are present earlier in the summer.

▶ **Getting There:** Cairns is served by a number of carriers, including Qantas, American, and United. Flights from the United States generally depart from Los Angeles.

▶ **Accommodations:** Cairns is a sophisticated city of 120,000 residents and it offers numerous hotel options. Visit www.tropicalaustralia.com.au to view a comprehensive list of accommodations.

▶ **Equipment:** Most fly anglers do not have sitting in the closet the kind of tackle neces-sary for billfish: 9-foot 12- to 14-weight rods and large-capacity reels are required. Dual hook flashy profile flies, large multihackled poppers, and tube flies can all be effective; if the fish is eager and the bait-and-switch is executed properly, as long as the fly is big enough it shouldn't matter much. There are several outfitters in Cairns that specialize in fly fishing for black marlin. These include Kim Andersen Sportfishing (+61 7 40 54 22 22; www.kimandersensportfishing.com) and Fishing Cairns (+61 7 40 38 11 44; www.fishingcairns.com.au). They can provide needed gear and help you execute the delicate choreography needed to seduce a billfish.

BONEFISH OFF
NORTH ANDROS ISLAND

RECOMMENDED BY **Brian O'Keefe**

The rich lore of bonefishing on North Andros pulls almost as powerfully as the present possibilities of the island's endless flats. North Andros served as an incubator for nascent gray-ghost fly-fishing efforts half a century ago and was home to the Bang Bang Club and the Lighthouse Club – two of the earliest bonefish lodges. Wall Street Brahmins sailed south on their yachts to hire Bahamians to help them hunt elusive bones, and the angling literati of the day – Lee Wulff, Joe Brooks, and the like – followed closely on their heels. The fishery has stood the test of time. (And remnants of the past are returning; Charlie Smith, creator of the Bonefish Charlie fly, has abetted the reincarnation of the long-defunct Bang Bang Club.) Despite North Andros's iconic place on the world list of bonefishing hot spots, it's still quite possible to find a stretch of flats to enjoy by yourself.

OPPOSITE:
North Andros
Island offers
seemingly
endless bone-
fish flats.

Andros Island is the largest of the Bahamas Islands, measuring one hundred miles long by forty miles wide, and is divided into three smaller islands: North, Middle, and South Andros. Each island is separated by a bight – a broad channel where tidal waters ebb and flow. Where the North Bight merges with the Middle, hundreds of flats have been formed, a veritable tropical paradise. On the northern end of the island you'll find Joulters' Cays, twenty more miles of bonefish flats. To the west lies a vast wilderness area, where flats and creeks are rarely fished, let alone named. All told, Andros offers more fishable bonefish flats than any region of the Caribbean. The predictability of the fishes' routines lets anglers (more accurately, their guides) target their preference – lots of small-er fish or shots at big fish.

The bonefish of Andros are legendary for their great size. In his wonderful book *Bonefishing!*, bonefish pioneer Randall Kaufmann says of the Middle Bight and the west coast, "Anglers tell of getting fifteen-pound, even twenty-pound bonefish to eat their fly and setting up hard on them four or five times before the fish just spit out the hook. They talk about losing fly line and two hundred fifty yards of backing on the first run...."

While the revamped Bang Bang Club and several other lodges stand at your service, the adventurous Brian O'Keefe prefers to travel à la carte. "We use Nicholls Town as our base. It's a small place with a few hotels, a great pub called the Big Shop that looks like Hollywood's idea of a Bahamian pub, and a little grilled-fish place, the Sly Fox, where you can get a conch salad that's just unbelievable. The places we stay are pretty basic but clean and friendly. We're not in the room too much." On a typical day, Brian will have a fruit plate for breakfast, put on his wading booties and fanny pack, and meet up with his favorite guide – a fellow named Philip Rolle – to discuss options. These are generally dictated by the weather. If it's calm, they'll run over to west Andros. It's about an hour and a half ride, but very worthwhile. It's a saltwater wilderness; the west side is uninhabited, so you won't see any development over there, and not many other boats. On west Andros, they'll focus on bones and tarpon. Jacks, snapper, and barracuda are also available in the deep-water cuts. A floating line covers all situations here well. "The beauty is, you never know what will happen next," Brian continued. "We might see one-hundred-fifty-pound tarpon rolling, or baby tarpon in the twenty-pound class. Almost every flat has bonefish. It's constant action and constant variety."

If the weather is breezy, Brian and Philip will probably do a standard bonefish trip to the Joulters. Joulters' Cays consists of a smattering of low, sandy islands and a long string of flats, all wadeable. The boat is used to get from spot A to spot B; most of the fishing is done from the flats. "At Joulters, we work the tides to our advantage," Brian said. "If we catch things right, we can get in six good fishing hours. Philip has an excellent sense of when and where fish are coming and going. Some of the fish we're casting to are in the thirty-inch range; fish of four to five pounds are average. During downtime, we might go for shark, permit, or snapper. Snapper can make a great dinner. When I'm there, I feel like a kid. There's always something happening. On the way back into town, we usually try to leave time to snorkel a coral head or two. To only fish and not get into that beautiful water seems a shame."

In his slightly younger days, Brian passed on the motel in Nicholls Town altogether and roughed it out on the Joulters – that is, until some uninvited guests showed up. "We'd built a permanent but very bare-bones camp on one of the islands. It was like something out of *Gilligan's Island*. It was literally a five-foot walk to begin fishing. We're there with an inflatable kayak and little else. One night, we heard a good deal of ruckus out in the ocean. There was the beating of helicopters and the flashing of flares. I figured that either some big boat hit the reef or it's a drug bust. We went back to sleep. A half hour later, our camp was under attack by a Black Hawk helicopter. Apparently, they mistook us for drug smugglers. Everything was airborne – our kayak, our tarp, our cooking stuff. They completely trashed our camp. This was pretty scary. I learned that you don't want to mess with the DEA."

Even the rather rude intrusion of the narcs can't displace Brian's most vivid memory of Andros. "In the evening, the sun has an orange glow. There are times when the tide is just right, and the bonefish spread out, and there are pods of bonefish as far as the eye can see. There might be more than a thousand tailing bonefish spread out over a couple miles of flats. It shows the amazing potential of a good, healthy flat. When the bonefish tail, their tails sometimes take on the orange glow."

BRIAN O'KEEFE has fished and photographed the world. His photographs have appeared in the *Los Angeles Times*, the *New York Times*, *USA Today*, *Men's Journal*, and just about every fishing magazine you can imagine. In addition to his photography work, Brian is a tackle rep for Scientific Anglers, Scott Fly Rods, and Chota Wading Boots and Waders. He is also a Master Certified Fly Casting Instructor from the Federation of Fly Fishers (FFF). See Brian's photography at www.brianokeefephotos.com.

IF YOU GO

▶ **Prime Time:** The east coast of Andros fishes best October through January. The west coast fishes best February through August.

▶ **Getting There:** Andros Island is located approximately 150 miles southeast of Miami. Visitors generally fly to Miami or Nassau, and then arrange a flight to Andros Town. Air Charter Bahamas (866-FLY-ISLANDS; www.aircharterbahamas.com) and Yellow Air Taxi (888-YELLOW-4; www.flyyellowairtaxi.com) both provide service.

▶ **Accommodations:** While the largest island of the Bahamas chain, Andros is the least populated, and it has somewhat limited accommodations. Green Windows Inn (242-329-2194) in Nicholls Town offers decent motel-style digs. There are a number of fly-fishing lodges on Andros, including Mangrove Cay, Andros Island Fishing Club, and the Bang

Bang Club (866-712-7303; www.bahamasfish.com). A seven-night/six-day fishing package at one of the lodges (including lodging, meals, and guides) will run in the vicinity of $3,000. For a more comprehensive list of hotels and lodges, visit www.bahamas.com.

► **Equipment:** For Andros bonefish, you'll want a 9-foot 7- or 8-weight rod equipped with floating line and a minimum of 150 yards of backing; 9-foot leaders tapered to 0x with tippet in 8- to 12-pound test will do fine. Standard bonefish flies produce well, including Crazy Charlies, Clouser Deep Minnows, Gotchas, and Brown Snapping Shrimp in #2–#8. For tarpon and permit, load up with a 9-foot 9- or 10-weight rod. Have floating line for permit, intermediate and fast-sinking lines for tarpon, all outfitted with at least 200 yards of backing. For permit, you'll need a 9-foot leader ending in 15-pound tippet; for tarpon, the same setup, plus an 80-pound shock tippet. Deceivers, Black Death, and Cockroach patterns in #1/0-#3/0 work for tarpon. McCrab, Del's Permit Crab, and Expoxy flies are good permit choices. Brian's favorite guide, Philip Rolle, can be booked through Mark Summers at 800-694-4162.

PEACOCK BASS ON THE
RIO NEGRO RIVER

RECOMMENDED BY **Pat Pendergast**

Peacock bass are one of the few fish that are celebrated as much for their great sporting potential on a fly rod as for their ability to *bust* a fly rod. Their pugnacious nature is drawing more and more anglers to the Amazonian rain forests and Brazil's Rio Negro.

Peacocks are not bass at all but members of the cichlid family, a cousin of the oscar. The fish sport a black patch directly behind the eye and three vertical black bars. There are several varieties of peacocks in the Rio Negro system, and they all share the same ornery temperament and explosive fighting ability.

"My first trip there was like entering into a Tarzan movie," Pat Pendergast remembered. "We jumped on a Cessna Caravan in Manaus [staging area for many Amazonian expeditions] outfitted with pontoons, and took off over the jungle. For an hour and fifteen minutes it was nothing but dense jungle as we flew five or six thousand feet overhead. Then there was suddenly a small clearing and a river, and then a flotilla of barges, attached to an old-style riverboat. We landed and taxied up to the procession. On each barge was a Weatherport tent, complete with electricity and a bathroom. This would be home for the next week. Not bad for the middle of the jungle!"

The floating caravan gives the peacock-bass adventure an expedition feel. It also allows anglers to follow the fish. Water levels play a key role in stalking peacock bass – in most cases, the lower the better. "When water levels are high during the rainy season, the peacock bass are spread out throughout the jungle, wherever the flood plain extends. When the water recedes, the fish move back into the river channel and the lagoons that formed. They're more concentrated and, naturally, the fishing greatly improves."

Anglers board smaller craft and cruise down the river, looking for coves or inlets that cut back into the jungle and for sandbars and rock outcroppings. The fish tend to congregate around such areas to wait in ambush for prey. At times, a given tributary might be clear enough to allow sight fishing. More often than not, waters colored by suspended silt and tannins compel anglers to blind-cast to promising lies. While modestly long casts are sometimes required, Amazon anglers needn't worry about matching the hatch. Peacocks are not finicky eaters. If the water is clear, they will take poppers on the surface; if it's murky, you'll fare better with streamers. Large-profiled patterns tied on high-quality stainless steel hooks in large sizes – 3/0 and 4/0s – work best. A fast, erratic retrieve is effective. When the strike comes, you'll know it. "Peacocks are incredibly fast and superaggressive," Pat recalled. "Sometimes we'd be floating along and see a rainbow streak. That would be a peacock. You can't imagine how hard they hit a fly. At one point, we had one guy fishing a saltwater plug on conventional gear. Several fish hit so hard that they crushed the plugs, which were made of strong plastic. Crushed them! I have to describe angling for peacock bass as combat fishing. They're so strong, and there are so many holes along the shoreline for them to charge into and break you off, you have to try and muscle them out. They're incredibly acrobatic. By the end of the week, I was black and blue from jamming the rod into my stomach."

There have been tales of some epic weeks on the Rio Negro system. One report claimed more than 1,200 fish caught among six anglers in one week, with fish reaching weights of 19 pounds. Exaggeration? Not at all. "Given low water conditions, good anglers can expect to hook between twenty and thirty-five or more peacocks a day, landing about half," Pat reported. "Some anglers get into a hundred or more fish in one day. Most fish average between four and six pounds."

The flora and fauna of the Amazon complete the Rio Negro experience. Birders will appreciate the variety of avian life, including toucans, parakeets, and parrots. Monkeys, tapirs, and paca (a species of large rodent) are frequently encountered; one may even cross paths with a jaguar. Some wildlife is encountered on a more intimate basis ... that is, on a plate. "During my trip, we had the chance to sample local fare. We ate tapir, paca, and occasionally a peacock bass that had been injured. Peacocks are excellent eating. One night, we ate piranha soup – a little strong and oily for my taste, like *menudo*."

Most visitors have a few spare hours in Manaus, which is an experience in itself. "It's like something out of a James Bond movie," Pat said. "Especially the city's open-air market. People are paddling in from deep in the jungle with dugout canoes filled with fruit and live pigs. Riverboats that could have sailed straight out of *Huckleberry Finn* are pulled up to the docks, along with the canoes and more modern craft. You can buy anything, from monkey flesh to bootlegged tapes to Lord knows what. The collision of old and new and the utterly bizarre leaves you wondering, 'Where am I? What year am I in?'"

PAT PENDERGAST is director of International Travel at The Fly Shop, headquartered in Redding, California. His fishing adventures have taken him to Alaska, Argentina, Chile, Mexico, Honduras, Venezuela, Brazil, the Bahamas, Belize, Christmas Island, French Polynesia, Russia, Canada, and more. Before joining The Fly Shop, Pat guided anglers in Alaska for five years, where he also ran a sportfishing camp.

IF YOU GO

▶ **Prime Time:** The Rio Negro region is fishable through the dry months – mid-September through mid-March. Late winter can offer the lowest water, and some of the best fishing.

▶ **Getting There:** U.S. anglers generally depart from Miami on a red-eye flight to Manaus, Brazil, which is served by several airlines, including Lloyd Aero Boliviano. A floatplane will deliver you from Manaus to your rendezvous with the barge flotilla.

▶ **Accommodations:** The barge trip described by Pat Pendergast (outfitted by Rio Plate Anglers) offers great mobility, which translates into the quickest access to fish. A self-contained riverboat, the *Amazon Angel*, offers a similar program. If you'd prefer to dwell on dry land, consider the Rio Negro Lodge. The price for a week's angling with any of these outfitters is in the neighborhood of $3,500. All of these outfitters provide air transportation to the river from Manaus and back, all meals and beverages, and guides. While guides are not always fluent English speakers, they do feel comfortable with "fishing English."

▶ **Equipment:** To combat peacocks, you need a strong stick: a 9-foot 9- to 11-weight rod is preferred. Bring a few extra rods – peacocks bust rods *often*. Reels should be outfitted with floating line, an intermediate sinking line, and, for the rare occasions when the fish are down, a Teeny 300 line. Bring tropical lines – they can endure the heat. Two hundred yards of backing should suffice. A shock tippet of 30- to 40-pound mono-filament will work for your leader. Poppers, Dahlberg Divers, Lefty's Deceivers, and Clouser Minnows in a variety of colors, tied on 3/0 and 4/0 hooks, will bring the big boys on.

STEELHEAD ON THE DEAN RIVER

RECOMMENDED BY **Tony Hayes**

Just how good is the steelhead fishing on British Columbia's Dean River? Tony Hayes gives it the ultimate praise: "Simply look at how many fly-shop owners and fly-fishing lodge owners are actually willing to pay real money to go up there!"

The Dean River slices through the Coast Mountains east of Bella Coola, carving deep canyons that are framed by steep mountains and towering glaciers as the river rushes to the sea. The glacial origins of the river and its tributaries give the Dean a perpetual tint that can dictate angling techniques. The river's powerful current (fish have to overcome several falls on the lower river), the freshness of the fish from the ocean, and the fact that the fish enter the river during warmer water temperatures all account for the Dean steelhead's incredible fighting prowess. Many steelhead aficionados who have chased chromers far and wide consider Dean River fish – some of which reach 30 pounds – to be the mightiest of them all.

For Tony, fishing the Dean for steelhead is a homecoming of sorts to his beloved Tongariro River and Lake Taupo in New Zealand. "A century ago, steelhead stock were introduced to Lake Taupo from the Russian River, north of San Francisco. The fish have thrived in New Zealand. Their migratory instincts take them up rivers to spawn. Though they're not technically steelhead, they are bright silver fish, similar, I suppose, to Great Lakes steelhead, though a bit smaller. Fishing the Dean is like going back to the roots of the Taupo fishery. I'm very attracted to the idea of catching sea-run rainbows in B.C., the capital of steelhead fishing."

Anglers did not recognize the sport-fishing potential of the Dean until the mid-1950s, largely because of its secluded nature; it could be accessed only by floatplane or horse. (In the previous century, the canyon and mouth of the Dean barely escaped becoming the

OPPOSITE:
The Coast
Mountains rise
abruptly from
the Dean,
providing a
dramatic
backdrop for
steelheaders.

49

western terminus of the transcontinental route of the Canadian Pacific Railway; fishing would likely have suffered.) In the early 1960s, logging roads were built into the Dean, increasing access, though fortunately not decimating the water quality. Logging permits still exist for the Dean, though the area is being considered for protected status.

There are two distinct segments of the Dean: the lower section, from tidewater to the lower canyon, about two miles up from the Pacific; and the upper section, which encompasses the river above the lower canyon up to Crag Creek. The lower section fishes best from late June through July, when the two runs of summer fish that reach these waters (one that spawns in the Takia River, the other that spawns in the Dean) are charging through from the salt. These powerful fish are at their feisty peak in the canyon.

August and September are the best months to fish the upper section. There are several lodges on the upper Dean, though many seasoned anglers prefer to float the river, which affords a great wilderness experience, replete with grizzlies.

Wilderness is good, of course, but for Tony the wildness of Dean River fish is even better. "The last time I fished the Dean, my friends and I did embarrassingly well. On one day we landed about five fish each. A few were over twenty-four pounds. Near the end of the trip, I was fishing a long run, not far from the old concrete bridge pier. I hooked a fish in there, a good one. I played him for fifteen or twenty minutes and, for the life of me, I couldn't hold him. A mate came up with the raft and we floated through two rapids – two hundred yards or more – with the fish still pumping. Finally, we came to a swirling pool. I thought I had him in that calm water. Just as we were getting him to the bank, he spit the fly. I won't forget that battle soon."

To find success on the Dean, anglers must be sensitive to changes in water clarity and temperature. In his book *Steelhead River Journal: Dean*, Art Lingren points out five factors to consider: to what depth can you see in the river; what is the temperature, velocity, and surface turbulence of the water; what are light conditions – is it sunny, cloudy, or is the water shaded; what is the time of day; and are the fish fresh-run or have they been in the river for some time? If the water is cold and murky, a sink-tip line and a large fly (up to size 5/0!) may be necessary to reach the fish and be seen. If the water temperatures are warmer, the water has good visibility, and the sun is not bright overhead, a skated fly might produce. "Overall, the wet-fly fishing was quite similar to the Tongariro," Tony recalled, "except we needed to slow the fly down a bit more. It's vital to have a tight line throughout the drift. The strike of the fish was different. I had to constantly remind myself *not* to instantly set the hook when a fish took the fly. I'd say that my most memorable take on the Dean came with a floating line. I was fishing a wet fly when a fish rolled not fifteen feet in front of me. I didn't have any steelhead dry flies per se, though I did have a Royal Wulff. That was good enough – the fish took on the second or third cast!"

TONY HAYES became hooked on fly fishing more than forty years ago. He has been guiding in the Lake Taupo region of the North Island of New Zealand since 1977 and helped set up the world-famous Tongariro Lodge, which he co-owns, in 1981. Tony has fished all over the world, including in Russia, South America, Christmas Island, Mexico, and Fiji. His favorite fishing experience, however, remains pursuing steelhead on the rivers of British Columbia.

IF YOU GO

▶ **Prime Time:** Anglers targeting fish in the lower river should time their trips for July. Anglers on the upper river will find the best fishing late July through early September. Contact the Cariboo Fish and Wildlife Regional Office at 250-398-4530 about permits for unguided angling.

▶ **Getting There:** Dean River anglers generally use Bella Coola, B.C., as a staging area and reach their lodge or put-in place (for floaters) by jet boat or helicopter. Air service from Vancouver to Bella Coola is offered by Air Canada.

▶ **Accommodations:** On the lower river, there's Nakia Lodge (250-339-6681); up from the canyon, there's Hodson's Camp and Lower Dean River Lodge (www.lowerdean.com). All-inclusive weeklong packages (lodging, food, guides) at these camps are about $4,500. Slots are limited. Some camping spots are available in the first five miles of river.

▶ **Equipment:** The Dean will demand some longer casts and the fish are very strong, hence a 9-weight rod is recommended; many anglers use spey outfits to get extra distance and better line control. Your reels should be loaded with floating-, medium sink-tip, and fast sink-tip lines, and at least 200 yards of backing. Reliable wet flies include Popsicles in orange, red, and purple (#2–#5/0); General Practitioner in black (#2–#5/0); and Black Spey (#2–#6). For skaters, stock your box with Greased Liners, Bombers, and Steelhead Bees, in sizes #1/0 through #6.

STEELHEAD ON THE SKEENA SYSTEM

RECOMMENDED BY **Lani Waller**

For die-hard steelheaders, British Columbia is Valhalla. And if this heaven on earth has a central artery, it is the Skeena River and its tributary rivers, rivers that Lani Waller has plied for more than thirty years.

"The Skeena system is simply the best assortment of steelhead rivers in the world," Lani said. "There's something for everyone. Some rivers have road access, some you have to hike to, some you have to fly or float into. The Mother Skeena is a frighteningly huge river. Fishing there is like standing on the edge of the universe – you feel like an ant. On the other hand, the Copper and upper Kispiox have a face-to-face intimacy. You have the illusion of being as big as the river. Together, the Skeena presents a matrix of opportunity that's found nowhere else in the world. Each river is different, yet each shares a common thread." It should be noted, too, that each is quite capable of producing the next world-record steelhead.

A list of the Skeena tributaries reads like a who's who of steelhead rivers: the Babine, the Bulkley, the Copper, the Kispiox, the Morice, the Sustut. The Kispiox, Babine, and Sustut are known for yielding especially large steelhead, fish approaching 40 pounds (fish on these rivers average near 15 pounds); the fish of the Bulkley and the Morice are prized for being "players" – fish that will rise eagerly to a dry fly. When fall arrives, steelheaders descend on the small town of Smithers to plot their piscine assaults on the estimated 30,000 to 40,000 wild fish that enter the Skeena system between late August and November. If one river is blown out (which happens more often than anglers with short fishing vacations would like), chances are there's another river within striking distance that's still fishing well.

For Lani, each steelhead encounter is intensely personal, like this one on the Babine.

OPPOSITE:
The rivers of the Skeena system regularly yield the world's largest steelhead.

DESTINATION 10

"The water was off-color on this particular day, with a visibility of perhaps twenty-four inches," Lani recalled. "I was curious to see if I could raise a fish. I made a cast near shore, not more than ten or fifteen feet. A shadow like a zeppelin began to lift in the water. It was a female I estimated at thirteen pounds. I could see her eyes focusing on the fly. She moved toward the fly and took it. I didn't set the hook. The fish began slowly sinking down. She seemed to realize that something was wrong. I watched her slowly open her mouth and let the fly out. She had an expression on her face – curiosity, or perhaps revulsion. It's at moments like these that I seriously consider the possibility of sentiment in a trout."

While all Skeena-system steelhead will take a skated dry fly at times, it's the "players" in the Morice and Bulkley that have gained notoriety for their willingness to attack surface patterns. (The Morice is actually the upper section of the Bulkley; when the smaller upper Bulkley meets the Morice, the larger river becomes the Bulkley.) Writer/angler Ian Forbes speculates that the Morice/Bulkley steelheads' fondness for dry flies develops from feeding on the Bulkley's rich insect life in their formative smolt years. The memory of surface insects is imprinted in the brain, a muscle memory of sorts. Often, steelhead will rise to a skated fly numerous times, even bumping it with the snout, before taking it. Such behavior seems almost playful ... and this goes back to the notion of steelhead personality. "When conditions are right, fishing a dry fly can be the easiest way to take a steelhead," Lani ventured. "You know when you're making a mistake, because you can see everything – when there's too much drag in your presentation, or if you set the hook too soon. When one of these big fish breaks through the surface like a shark, it doesn't get any more exciting. If the water temperature is between fifty and sixty degrees and fairly clear, I'll fish dries on any of the Skeena rivers."

Wild steelhead tend to frequent wild, untrammeled places, and running amok amid the mountains and valleys of north-central British Columbia is part of the pleasure of a Skeena steelhead experience. Fly fishing for steelhead is always a crapshoot; while some of the remote lodges boast decent catch rates, anglers fishing the public water could enjoy multifish days or zero-fish weeks. (The uncertainty of the endeavor is one of steelheading's perverse appeals.) Pause on the riverbank and look for grizzly tracks among the decaying salmon carcasses. Watch the play of the golden leaves of the aspens and cottonwoods against the dark greens of dense spruce stands. Think about the thousands of miles the steelhead have traveled to come home.

"Steelhead inspire romance, in the fullest sense of the word," Lani mused. "They inspire it in a way that no other fish do. It's something in their journey, in what they endure. They're hard workers, they're warriors. They're also beautiful."

LANI WALLER has been fly fishing for forty-five years and was inducted into the Federation of Fly Fishers' Hall of Fame in 1997. His articles and stories have appeared in all the major fly-fishing publications and he serves as consultant to Sage Rod Co., Scientific Anglers 3M, and Umpqua Feather Merchants. He is the West Coast field editor for *Fly Fisherman* and his three 1984 award-winning videos done on steelhead fishing for Scientific Anglers 3M have become classics. Lani is the owner of Worldwide Anglers travel service, which specializes in B.C. steelhead fishing.

IF YOU GO

► **Prime Time:** Fish enter the Skeena system from mid-August through November. A visit from mid-September through mid-October will generally offer good fishing on the greatest number of Skeena rivers, providing that the fall rains hold off.

► **Getting There:** Smithers, the base camp for many Skeena-system adventures, is approximately six hundred miles north of Vancouver. If you plan to fish on your own, you'll need a car. Air Canada offers commercial air service from Vancouver to Smithers.

► **Accommodations:** The town of Smithers offers accommodations ranging from campgrounds and motels to bed-and-breakfasts; see options at www.tourismsmithers.com. Several well-respected lodges operate in the area. On the Babine, there's Silver Hilton Lodge (415-897-4997; www.wwanglers.com/shlodge.htm). On the Sustut, there's Steelhead Valhalla Lodge (250-847-9351; www.steelheadvalhallalodge.com) and Suskeena Lodge (250-847-9233; www.fishtourcanada.bc.ca). All-inclusive packages (air transportation from Smithers, food, guides) are in the vicinity of $3,500 to $4,000. Space is very limited, especially on peak weeks.

► **Equipment:** Skeena-system fish can push and exceed 20 pounds, which recommends rods in the 8- to 10-weight class. On the bigger rivers, spey rods facilitate longer casts. Bring floating line and type IV sink-tip, plus at least 100 yards of backing. Most standard steelhead wet flies will work, in #4 to #1/0. For dries, bring Bombers, Waller Wakers, Humpies, and Bulkley Mouse, in #2 through #8.

BROWN AND RAINBOW TROUT
AROUND GREATER REDDING

RECOMMENDED BY **Shane Kohlbeck** AND **Mike Mercer**

From the perspective of a car cruising along Interstate 5, the northern California town of Redding does not immediately conjure up the phrase "fly fisherman's paradise." Yet to the east and north of the city limits – and for that matter, within a stone's throw of downtown – run a dizzying array of trout streams. Spring creeks. Free stones. Tailwaters. Countless tiny mountain streams teeming with native rainbows. "I keep thinking I should write an article describing Redding as a fly-fishing destination," Mike Mercer ventured. "But then selfish motivations take over, and it never gets written."

Many of the rivers of Redding hold venerable spots in the canon of western fly waters: the Upper Sacramento, the McCloud, the Pit, the Fall, Hat Creek. For some of the biggest fish the area offers, cognoscenti know there's no need to look further than the Lower Sacramento, an intimidating flow that parallels the Interstate at times, and bifurcates Redding. "Last year, I caught two wild rainbows in the Lower Sac that each topped ten pounds," recalled Shane Kohlbeck. "The amazing thing was, I got them under city street bridges." Since the state of California began more closely monitoring the release of cold water from the dam that forms Lake Shasta, there's been a resurgence of insect life in the river. "We can have some tremendous surface action in the first few weeks of March fishing caddis patterns. Caddis hatches are also pretty reliable the last hour or two before dark during the summer. From October through the winter, Blue-Winged Olives are pretty constant. When the salmon arrive in October, we sight-fish to 'bows stacked up behind chinook redds, with egg patterns." There don't seem to be many small fish in the Lower Sac; rainbows average 15 to 18 inches, and there are many fish in the 5- to 10-pound class. When water levels are lower, the Lower Sac can be selectively waded. To cover the most water, many anglers fish from a drift boat.

OPPOSITE:
The flats below
Power House
#2 on Hat
Creek are one
of western
fly fishing's
great testing
grounds.

For a very different experience, Shane enjoys the pocket water of the Pit, a fairly primitive river with a unique strain of feisty rainbows. "We've nicknamed it the greased bowling ball river," Shane quipped. "It's wading-staff territory, even for the young and athletic angler. It's gotten a little more pressure in the last few years, but if a guy can hike some rugged terrain for twenty minutes, he can get to good water, and some privacy. The fish are very scrappy – they really get airborne. And they aren't terribly selective. There will be some good hatches on the Pit, but I generally high-stick nymph with a tiny indicator."

Moving a bit south and east from the Pit is Hat Creek, a spring creek not known for its solitude. Many fly fishers have seen photographs of anglers queued along the grass-lined flats below the Power House #2 riffle, casting tiny mayfly and midge imitations on fine tippets to native rainbows that have seen it all. While this technical fishing defines the Hat Creek experience for many, Mike Mercer likes the riffle water on the lower third of the wild trout area. "When I guided more often, the lower riffle was often my ace in the hole. Only a small percentage of the riffles hold fish, and it's not terrifically obvious which ones. The holding positions in those riffles were also very specific, right at the top of the trough. You could be five steps one way or another and not catch anything. Through trial and error, I got to know it well. I could take a complete novice down there and catch a half dozen thirteen- to eighteen-inch fish, mostly on Green Drake and golden stone nymphs. A lot of people don't realize that fish down there will key on salmonflies in the late spring. Near the top of the riffles, I'll fish salmonfly dries under the trees. The fish are there."

Moving north again, you'll come to Fall River, one of the biggest (and, to many, one of the best) spring creeks in the West. The fertile Fall fosters rich insect populations that support fat, native rainbows that regularly top 20 inches. Most anglers approach the Fall in prams, as extensive private property and a weed-choked bottom make wading difficult.

"The fish are very surface-conscious, and very particular – though not necessarily easily put down," Mike commented. "In its own way, it's every bit as good as Henry's Fork, especially for the angler who's a dry-fly connoisseur. Technique is a little different on the Fall. You cast downstream to rising fish and feed line until the fly goes over the fish. You need to position the fly to go *right* over the fish or they won't take. I've tried fishing upstream, but it didn't work very well. In my opinion, everyone should fish the Fall at least once, as it's so dramatically different in character from the region's other rivers."

Winding south and west from the Fall, you'll reach the McCloud, whose rainbow spawn have been transplanted throughout the world. The Lower McCloud is of primary interest to fly anglers for its native rainbows and migratory browns that can top 10 pounds as well as for its terrific beauty. "The canyons of the McCloud stay lush and green, even in the heat of the summer," Mike marveled. "What we hear a lot is, 'Boy, I got beat up fishing there, but it sure was beautiful.'" The McCloud is not easy fishing, thanks in part to heavy water, steep riverbanks, and slick wading, but there are times when it fishes easier than others. "Fishing mayfly nymphs with a small indicator in the mid-spring produces extremely well for rainbows. It's as close to a slam-dunk as you'll get on the McCloud. If you hook twenty fish, two will be close to eighteen inches. A lot of people come up in October hoping to hook into one of those big browns on October caddis, which is a prominent hatch. I've never had much luck with caddis dries. Streamers can work well, though I prefer to fish small nymphs in tailouts where I can spot fish. Even if the fishing is slow, the fall colors are beautiful."

With so many opportunities available, what would make a perfect trouting day in Redding? For Mike Mercer it would go like this: "Let's find a sunny day in late spring, when we have lots of insects coming off. I'd get an early start and hit the flats on Hat Creek and fish the Pale Morning Dun spinner fall hatch from eight to ten. Then I'd run down to the riffles and fish green drake nymphs for an hour, and then hit the upper section of the riffles and toss salmon flies up under the trees for an hour. By noon, I'm heading back to Redding. I'd pick up a big burger at Bartel's Giant Burger, then launch my drift boat on the Lower Sac at Posse Grounds. I'd fish caddis pupae for big rainbows, all sixteen to twenty inches. If I put in at two P.M., I'd take out by six. Next, I'd head north to the Upper Sac. The river is coming back well since the pesticide spill in 1990. I'd nymph from eight to nine, then fish caddis dries to the big snouts that would be coming up at that time. When the golden stones come off at dark, I'd tie on a salmonfly and cast in the direction of the dropping-bowling-ball sounds. Then it's an hour home." Sleep shouldn't come hard after such a day. And what sweet dreams!

SHANE KOHLBECK has worked for The Fly Shop since 1997 and currently serves as director of guide services. He began fly fishing at age nine, and today he focuses his efforts on the Lower and Upper Sacramento, Trinity, and Pit rivers. He's fished in Los Roques, Venezuela; the Yucatán; British Columbia, and Russia. Shane is a FFF Certified Casting Instructor and has taught numerous casting seminars with Mel Krieger.

MIKE MERCER has been with The Fly Shop for twenty-four of the store's twenty-five years of existence. He started as the stock boy and now manages The Fly Shop's Alaska Travel operations. Mike has fished many of the world's fly-fishing dream destinations and is recognized as one of the West's leading fly designers. He is an Umpqua Feather Merchants contract fly tier and many of his designs are being used successfully around the world.

IF YOU GO

▶ **Prime Time:** The largest concentration of insect activity occurs in June. While fishing slows a bit in the summer doldrums (greater Redding is one of the hottest regions in California), activity picks up again in the fall. The Lower Sacramento is open year-round.

▶ **Getting There:** Redding is 200 miles north of San Francisco, 160 miles north of Sacramento. The Lower Sac is in town; Hat Creek, the Pit, and Upper Sac are roughly an hour's drive away; Fall River and the McCloud are about two hours distant.

▶ **Accommodations:** If you choose to stay in Redding, most of the major chains are represented (see a list at www.reddingchamber.com). If you focus your efforts on the Hat and the Pit, you might opt to stay in Burney or Fall River Mills; the latter boasts a slightly upscale option, the Pit River Lodge (530-336-5005; www.pitriverlodge.com). Visitors focusing on the McCloud who don't camp on the river will find numerous accommodation options in the town of McCloud (www.mccloudchamber.com/lodging.html). On the Fall River, the preferred choice is the Riverside House (800-669-3474), which includes johnboats for fishing the Fall.

▶ **Equipment:** A 9-foot 5-weight rod outfitted with floating line and 100 yards of backing (especially for the Lower Sac) will satisfy most needs, though anglers may desire a more delicate rod for some situations, and a stiffer stick for the Lower Sac. Tippets and flies will vary depending on which rivers you decide to fish. Before you go, contact The Fly Shop (800-669-3474; www.theflyshop.com). It's a great shop, and the folks there really know the waters. Guide service is also available for all the area's rivers. Rates are $325 per day for two anglers, $410 per day for three.

BROWN AND RAINBOW TROUT
OFF CHILEAN FJORDS

RECOMMENDED BY **John Eustice**

When Chile's preeminent fly fisher, Adrian Dufflocq, asked John Eustice to take an exploratory fishing trip, Eustice knew a special adventure was about to unfold. "Back in 1993, Adrian and his sons, Cristian and Marcelo, hired a large yacht and we set out to explore the uninhabited fjords of southern Chile," John said. "When we set off from Port Cisnes, it was overcast and foggy. Pisco Sours (the unofficial cocktail of Chile) were prepared and passed around. After several rounds the fog cleared. We looked to the shore to see waterfalls cascading off the mountains. As night fell, the moon soon came out. Adrian pointed to another part of the sky and there was the Southern Cross. It was one of the most sublime moments of my life."

The fjords of southern Chile are among the most scenically spectacular areas of the world. Roadless and remote, it's a land where temperate rain forests climb the southern Andes to the snowfields and mingle with epic glaciers and volcanoes. The region is home to penguins, sea lions, albatross, and the rare Chilean black dolphin. Courtesy of stocking efforts in the early 1900s and more recent aquaculture escapees, the waters off Chile are also home to a grand assortment of salmonids. Rainbow trout came from Oregon, browns from Germany, and coho, king, and Atlantic salmon from the pens. The good news is that many of the introduced salmonids have evolved into naturally reproducing populations, and the untrammeled conditions of the southern Chilean watersheds have allowed the fish to grow quickly, with trout averaging 5 pounds in some drainages. Fishing the Chilean fjords tends to prompt many questions, such as: "Are the fish we're catching resident or sea-run? Are they steelhead or rainbows ... or coho? What's the name of this river? Where is the river?" Drawing on his experience, John Eustice can unravel a few of these mysteries.

"The program runs like this. You make your way down the coast, seeking out rivers that have been fished before with good results, or scouting out rivers that may have never been fished. When you come upon something that looks promising, it's into the Zodiacs with a guide and off to fish and explore. In some rivers, we had no idea if we'd catch anything. 'Small rivers with big surprises' is how Dufflocq likes to describe the streams. At one point, we pulled into a bay where a small stream was evident in the distance. As the tide went out, the boat was soon resting on its keel. Where the bay had been, there was now a river channel. We could see fish darting around in the water columns that were created when the fresh water of the river hit the salt water of the Pacific, feeding on crustaceans. The banks were covered with mussels. Not your typical trout stream."

Some of the rivers flowing into the fjords hold browns, some hold rainbows, and some hold both with a smattering of salmon. Part of the fun is that you never know what you're going to hook. And sometimes you don't even know exactly what you've hooked once you've landed it. If the exact genetic makeup of some of southern Chile's coastal salmonids is a matter of contention, few will debate the fish's strength. Brown, sea-run brown, rainbow, or what have you, these are hard-fighting fish, requiring 7-weight rods and the patience to endure a long battle. Fish over 10 pounds have been landed on every adventure, and the occasional presence of salmon of various strains make fish topping 20 pounds a distinct possibility.

On some streams, anglers will find good fishing near the mouth where the stream meets the salt. On others, better fishing might await farther upstream, which may be accessed by raft or on foot. Some anglers just prefer the trek upstream for the chance to fish waters that have never been fished by *anyone*. The odds are good you'll find willing trout either way, and they are excellent that you will find no other anglers. This is truly the frontier. Fishing the fjords is an adventure, albeit an adventure with many creature comforts. Home for the week is a fifty-three-foot yacht, with a skilled chef and a seasoned crew ... and a collection of choice Chilean wines to accompany dinner.

While there is occasional dry-fly fishing among the fjords, anglers focusing on subsurface patterns will generally catch more and bigger fish. The trout feed primarily on baitfish, crayfish, and nymphs, so streamers are the order of the day. Woolly Buggers and Muddlers fished down and across will produce strikes. The water is generally clear enough that you can follow the action.

"You'll fish a river, run into another fjord, spot a few rivers, decide to fish one, and then move along. Some of the rivers fish well, others less so. For me, part of the fun is the pioneering sense such a trip provides. And in the midst of all this incredible scenery that you have to yourself, you'll enjoy a five-star meal."

JOHN EUSTICE moved to San Francisco after graduating from Notre Dame and pursued various careers in the business world while spending free moments fishing in Shasta County. Active in California Trout, John received a Streamkeeper Award for conservation efforts. He has served as a trustee for the American Museum of Fly Fishing, is a founding member of Oregon Trout, and is also a member of the North Umpqua Foundation. Since establishing the booking agency John Eustice & Associates in 1988, John has traveled the world in search of superb fly-fishing experiences.

IF YOU GO

▶ **Prime Time:** While the season is open from mid-November through April, December through March tend to be peak fishing times.

▶ **Getting There:** Fjord travelers will stage in Santiago, then take a three-hour flight to the Balmaceda Airport (served by LanChile). From there, you'll be spirited off to the small town of Puerto Cisnes to board your yacht.

▶ **Accommodations:** Your floating home for the week is a fifty-three-foot Hatteras yacht, operated by Rios Azules (www.fly-fish-chile.com/fjords/fjords.html), which is owned by the Dufflocq family. The yacht is well appointed; you'll suffer little for comfort. You access the rivers in Zodiac rafts lowered from the yacht and piloted by seasoned Chilean guides. A week's adventure (excluding airfare) runs approximately $5,400.

▶ **Equipment:** Some bring a number of rods to the fjords, ranging from 4- to 7-weights, though a 9-foot 7-weight outfit will tame the fjords' frisky fish and facilitate hucking big streamers. Your rod should be fitted with three lines: floating line, Teeny T-200, and a Type III sink-tip. You'll often need to fish deep, so don't forget the sinking lines. Bring 7-foot leaders in 0x and 1x, and 9-foot leaders tapered to 1x and 3x; tippet material in 1x through 4x will suffice. Popular flies include Muddler Minnow (#4); Girdle Bug (#6); Bead Head Woolly Bugger (#4); Bunny Leech (#6–#8) and Krystal Zonker (#4). Bring a few attractor dries too, such as Bombers (#6) and Royal Wulffs (#10).

BROWN AND RAINBOW TROUT
ON THE GUNNISON RIVER

RECOMMENDED BY **Joseph Daniel**

The Gunnison River in western Colorado begins at the junction of the East and Taylor rivers north of the town of Gunnison and reaches its terminus at the Colorado River near Grand Junction on the western side of the Continental Divide. The river has two distinct personalities: above Blue Mesa Reservoir, it's a freestone fishery, flowing through sub-alpine terrain; below Blue Mesa, the Gunnison carves its way through the steep and iso-lated canyons of Black Canyon National Park and Gunnison Gorge. The Gunnison boasts an incredibly rich biomass, qualifying it for Gold Medal status – Colorado's highest des-ignation for trout water. The river above Blue Mesa offers some excellent fishing, includ-ing a prodigious Green Drake hatch in the late spring. But it is the segment of the river flowing through Gunnison Gorge, and its salmonfly hatch, that holds special appeal for Joe Daniel.

The gorge – and, for that matter, Black Canyon upstream – is not a drive-up fishery. Vertical walls extend one thousand feet and more from rim to river. To access the gorge section, anglers must hike one of four trails from the canyon rim to reach the river. The easiest trail, Chukar, drops six hundred feet in the course of a mile; the other trails are more rigorous and limit all but the most agile anglers from fishing this stretch. The Chukar Trail is negotiable by horse, and this is a good thing; the horses will carry all the accoutrements for a float trip, which is the best way to experience this section of the Gunnison. "Like all good adventures, the Gunnison Gorge float has a rough entry," Joe said. "You come off the blacktop of I-Seventy, and suddenly you're driving across miles of muddy, rutted moonscape to reach the trailhead. Then it's a one-mile hike with all your gear straight down into an abyss. Just when it's beginning to hurt, you reach the river." The plunging cliffs, replete with soaring raptors, are an awesome sight to behold.

OPPOSITE: The steep canyons of Black Canyon National Park and the Gunnison Gorge limit access to the Gunnison, promising solitide.

This stretch of the Gunnison holds both rainbows and browns; though rainbows have taken a hit from whirling disease in the last decade, the 'bows that remain are hogs. Browns have taken up the slack in terms of numbers, and also reach 20-inch-plus proportions in the food-rich gorge. Both species have an affinity for salmonflies.

The western salmonfly (*Pteronarcys californica*) is cause for excitement on any of the western rivers where it emerges, and the Gunnison is no exception. They range in size from 2 inches to 3 inches long and boast an even longer wingspan. They take their name from a bright orange thorax and head. Salmonflies are serious protein; these bugs are big enough to disrupt traffic when they converge in serious numbers along rural roadways. On the Gunnison, salmonflies appear only in the lower section of the river, generally when water temperatures reach fifty degrees. The exact arrival of the salmonfly hatch is always a bit of a guessing game; if you hit it right, you can enjoy some absolutely epic dry-fly fishing. Joe's been on the river the past seven or eight years in early June, and his experience reveals June 9th to be the magic date. "If you're on the river at that time," he said, "you'll find the hatch somewhere. It really brings the big fish to the surface. This is one of the best opportunities you'll have to take twenty-inch fish on a dry fly."

Over time, Joe and his companions have been perfecting the Gunnison Gorge rock-wall drift. "The salmonflies are all over the walls, which extend right down into the river," Joe explained. "They'll run down the face of the rock, drop their eggs in the water, and run back up." The big fish are hanging right next to the ledge, waiting for Mrs. Salmonfly to make her deposit. "There's the sense that their backs must be touching the ledge," Joe continued. "You almost want your fly to stick to the wall – three inches away is too far. You don't have to see the fish rise to know where they are resting. Just look for splash marks, which might go six or eight inches up the wall. Drop your fly against the wall under a splash mark, you'll get a toilet-bowl strike. It will turn your world upside down."

The salmonfly hatch on the lower Gunnison can linger in stages of intensity for as long as four weeks, and good angling continues after the *P. californica* bacchanalia has subsided. Nymphing can be productive as the summer passes, though as the water warms anglers should be prepared to go progressively deeper. Big streamers pounded against the walls can also arouse the bigger fish from their August torpor. When the water cools in September, Gorge anglers will often return to the surface with hopper/dropper combos. Wise anglers will pull over at the riffles and focus quality angling time there on foot, as that's where the fish will be. One of the luxuries of a

Gunnison Gorge float is that you *have time* to pull over and fish the good water, and to take in the splendid isolation of one of the American West's great river corridors. With only thirteen miles to cover in three days, you can linger over breakfast in camp, take a few minutes to scan the cliff sides for bighorn sheep, and work through a promising run a second time. "The camping, the canyon, and the fishing are all wonderful," Joe said. "As float trips go, the quality of the Gorge experience is incredible."

JOSEPH DANIEL is the editor and publisher of the international fly-fishing travel magazine *Wild on the Fly* (www.wildonthefly.com). A Colorado native, Joe grew up fishing the trout-rich rivers of the Rockies. As a professional photographer and writer, he now travels the world reporting on new frontiers in angling, always in search of wild fish in wild waters.

IF YOU GO

▶ **Prime Time:** June is the best time to be on the Gunnison Gorge. Fishing is decent through the summer, though it's more subsurface oriented.

▶ **Getting There:** The put-in for floating the gorge is near Montrose, which is approximately 250 miles from Denver.

▶ **Accommodations:** Both Black Canyon Anglers (970-835-3962; www.blackcanyon anglers.com) and Gunnison River Expeditions (800-297-4441; www.cimarroncreek. com/flyfishing/ff_gre.html) offer three-day floats on the gorge. The cost is approximately $1,100 per person, based on double occupancy. The night before your expedition begins, consider a stay at Gunnison River Farms (970-835-3962; www.gunnisonriver farms.com), which is convenient to the put-in.

▶ **Equipment:** A 9-foot 5- or 6-weight rod equipped with a floating line and 100 yards of backing will work well on the Gunnison. Bring 9-foot leaders tapered to 3x through 5x, with tippet in 4- to 8-pound test. A variety of salmonfly imitations will work; if the fish are in a frenzied enough state almost anything big will produce. A few popular choices are Sofa Pillow, Bird's Stonefly, Double Humpy, and large yellow or orange Stimulators, in sizes #2 through #8. When the salmonfly season has passed, standard nymph patterns, such as Copper Johns, Princes, and Pheasant Tails (with beadheads) will work. Also bring some Woolly Buggers and Zonkers to cover streamer fishing.

TARPON OFF JARDINES

DE LA REINA

RECOMMENDED BY **John Ecklund**

An unintended boon of Fidel Castro's rise to power was the barring of visitors from Los Jardines de la Reina (the Queen's Gardens), a 150-mile-long archipelago located fifty miles off the southern coast of Cuba. Recognizing the region's rich marine life – and its potential for tourism – Castro's government designated the area (consisting of nearly a thousand square miles) a Cuban National Park in 1996. Closed to commercial fishing, and inhabitation, Los Jardines comprises one of the world's great protected saltwater wilderness areas, an area that in the past decade has become open to *very limited* sport-fishing through an Italian outfitter called Avalon. It's also the place where Pacific Northwest steelhead outfitter John Ecklund cut his teeth on tarpon.

"I've been visiting Cuba since it opened up for fishing, and I still can't get over the juxtaposition of the open blue waters and white sand of Los Jardines to the brown canyons and ponderosa pines of eastern Oregon. It's all sight-fishing down here, which is also a great departure from steelheading. The variety of available fishing options is incredible. Many visitors come down seeking bonefish, but then they see tarpon rolling all over, and their attention is piqued."

In terms of habitat and available species, Los Jardines has something for everyone. The 250 cays that make up the archipelago host mangrove swamps, coral flats, sand flats, and turtle-grass flats, all cut through with deep channels that deliver the fish into the shallows with the incoming tide. Bonefish are good-sized and plentiful, with 3- to 6-pound fish being average; anglers focusing on bones will likely have a shot at fish in the 8- to 10-pound class in the course of their visit. Wandering hundreds of miles of isolated flats casting to fish that have seen few, if any, other anglers, odds are high for some very productive fishing; twenty-bonefish days are not unheard of. Permits are also available in numbers considerable enough to give you a realistic shot at this enigmatic game fish. If you land a permit by midday, your chances of completing a coveted "Grand Slam" (permit, bonefish, and tarpon all on a fly) are astronomically high. Barracuda, jack crevalle, horse eye jacks, cubera, snapper, bonito kingfish, albacore, wahoo, and shark are also available. (The horse eyes make excellent sashimi, if your taste runs in that direction.) And then there are the tarpon.

Unlike some tarpon fisheries, which rely on migratory fish, Los Jardines has a considerable population of resident fish; it's believed that they live in huge rifts in the sea floor. Resident fish populations make locating fish to cast to a much easier task.

Several distinct groups of fish are available. "Baby" tarpon in the 10- to 40-pound class are present in the channels between the cays. Larger fish in the 45- to 80-pound class frequent the flats, and centennial fish (up to 130 pounds) can be found in a deeper ocean channel that Avalon guides have recently discovered.

"If I could catch one kind of fish all day, I would prefer the smaller fish in the thirty- to fifty-pound range," John confided. "They're much more acrobatic than the larger fish – a lot like steelhead, in that respect – and they don't wear me out as much. Still, even when I'm casting to a smaller fish, I have to take a deep breath to calm myself, so I don't melt. Seeing scores of fish on the flats on a calm morning is an unnerving experience.

"I've had some very fortunate fishing at Los Jardines, but on the most memorable week I jumped fifty-three fish. At one point, I had a fish of about forty-five pounds on. After several jumps, it threw the fly. As I was stripping it back, another fish took. I landed that one. Two tarpon on one cast – I think that says a lot about the tarpon numbers. If your fly's in the water, you're in the game."

The music of the Buena Vista Social Club has sent good Cuban vibrations around the world, and those who've made the trip to Los Jardines almost universally experience the same. The Cuban guides display wonderful hospitality, and the camaraderie between guests and staff is wonderful. Before the conclusion of each trip, there's a big party on the boat. The crew cranks up the music, mixes up some *mojitos* (the unofficial Cuban cocktail), and everyone dances as the sun sets. It's a wonderful way to end the trip.

JOHN ECKLUND operates Little Creek Outfitters (www.oregonrivers.com) and Hell's Canyon Whitewater Company, both based in La Grande, Oregon. He leads intrepid anglers on steelhead trips on the Grande Ronde and John Day rivers, and on trout-

14

DESTINATION

fishing and wine-tasting trips through Patagonia. An accomplished photographer, John has had his pictures published in Patagonia sales catalogs, *NW Steelheader* magazine, various Oregon tourism publications, and Randall Kaufmann's acclaimed book *Bonefishing*. He may be remembered best for his mojitos.

IF YOU GO

14

DESTINATION

▶ **Prime Time:** While fishing can be steady throughout the year, late April through the end of June tends to be the peak season.

▶ **Getting There:** North American citizens traveling to Cuba generally stage in Cancún, Mexico, which offers two flights a day to Havana. From there, another short flight, an hour-and-a-half drive to the small fishing town of Júcaro, and a three-and-a-half-hour boat trip will take you to your floating hotel. Your outfitter will help you navigate the morass of transfers and visas necessary to make the trip. If you've come this far and hanker for a taste of rich Cuban culture, tours of the mainland can also be arranged. (While presently it is still against the law for U.S. citizens to travel to Cuba without State Department preapproval, a certain number of Americans travel each year to Cuba without the U.S. government's blessing. If you go, you will be traveling at your own risk.)

▶ **Accommodations:** As you'll be fifty miles offshore, you'll have few options but to stay on one of the floating hotels operated by the Avalon Fishing Centre (www.avalons.net) – the *Halcon* or the *Tortuga*. Both boats provide comfortable surroundings and easy access to the unspoiled wonders of Los Jardines. Guests at Avalon will have hundreds of miles of flats to themselves, as there are no other outfitters operating in the Cuban National Park. If your arms wear out, there's first-class diving along the coral reefs on the south side of the archipelago. A week's fishing (including food, lodging, and guides) begins at $3,400.

▶ **Equipment:** Anglers fishing Cuba should have at least three rods: one for bonefish (7- or 8-weight), one for permit (8- or 9-weight), and one for tarpon (10- or 11-weight). Floating lines will do for bonefish. For permit and tarpon, floating and slow-sinking lines are needed; be sure to have plenty of backing (150 yards minimum for bonefish, 200 to 300 yards for tarpon and permit). A 9-foot to 12-foot tapered leader in sizes ranging from 10- to 15-pound test (for bonefish) and 12- to 16-pound (for permit) will do; for tarpon, you'll need a shock tippet of 60- to 80-pound mono. Standard fly patterns work well.

RAINBOW TROUT ON

BLAGDON LAKE

RECOMMENDED BY **Perk Perkins**

Mention England to a fly fisher and the chalkstreams of Hampshire will inevitably spring to mind. "Anglers who visit England should definitely fish a few of the chalkstreams," advised Perk Perkins, "but they shouldn't ignore the reservoirs." Perhaps the most celebrated of English reservoirs is Blagdon Lake.

Blagdon Lake is a 440-acre impoundment on the country's southwestern coast, near the city of Bristol. The reservoir was opened to angling in 1904, when it was decided by the lake's overseers (the Bristol Waterworks) that Blagdon would one day be a world-class fishery. A Scot named Donald Carr took the reins, supplementing native browns present from the River Yeo with stocked browns; rainbows were introduced shortly thereafter. Both species thrived, as did the fishery. Today, the lake is maintained as a put-and-take fishery, with generous stocking to boost catch rates. While many fish average between 3 and 5 pounds, holdover fish can reach impressive sizes; the best fish taken in 2002 was a 10-pound rainbow.

"There are reservoirs in England that have more fish and bigger fish," Perk said. "But the ambience of Blagdon is very special. The surrounding hillsides are picturesque, the way an American might picture the English countryside. Though it's a reservoir, Blagdon has the feeling of a natural lake." The techniques employed on Blagdon Lake are a great part of its appeal for Perk. "Generally speaking, the English are much more advanced on stillwater fishing techniques than Americans. This is the case for a simple reason: there are a limited number of trout streams, and almost all of that water is private. Lakes and reservoirs, on the other hand, are public, and get much more attention."

For most non-British anglers, loch-style fishing is extremely eye-opening and rewarding. It's completely different from the way Americans fish lakes. Anglers go out in a wooden dory and tie a sea anchor – somewhat like an umbrella – to the bottom of the boat. The sea anchor slows down the boat's drift. You try to drift broadside, with one angler in the bow and one in the stern. Anglers cast downwind, with a team of three flies. Generally, anglers will rig with a weighted damselfly on the point; a buzzer (the English term for a chironomid) on the middle, and a drowned caddis or mayfly on the uppermost fly. After casting, you'll strip the flies in just a little faster than the boat's drift, so you're not quite catching up to them. When your flies get closer, you turn your strip into a dapping motion. The breeze will catch line and lift it up, causing the flies to flutter near the surface. Many strikes come right at the boat.

"The first time I fished Blagdon was in 1982, when I was living in England managing Orvis's mail-order business," Perk continued. "A fellow named Chris Ogbourne [who's since gone on to captain the English national fly-fishing team] invited me to fish his home water. Chris was already considered one of England's great lake fly fishermen, so I was in good hands. When we got to the lake, it was very breezy. I was thinking, 'Bummer,' as in my lake fishing up to that point in the states, calm days were considered ideal, both for hatches and for spotting fish. Chris's response to the wind was an enthusiastic 'Brilliant.' They like a breezy day, as the fish will tend to rise upwind of their last rise as they follow the buzzers. If there's no breeze, their feeding is random. As we drifted along, Chris was spotting fish left and right. He would point and say, 'See that one? See that one?' and I'd say, 'No.' After forty-five minutes, I finally could make out what he was looking at – the tip of a dorsal fin jutting through the water. It was like a butter knife cutting through the waves. I gave a couple strips, and then the fish was on. The rainbows in Blagdon are very strong, very handsome chrome-colored fish. I'll always remember that fish, the excitement of being able to figure things out."

For Perk, the loch-fishing techniques nurtured on Blagdon have excellent application stateside. "I've been out on the Pothole Lakes in eastern Washington State, surrounded by guys in float tubes stripping Woolly Buggers. I'd get some funny looks as I drifted by in my canoe, dapping my three-fly rig, but it worked wonderfully." (It's worth noting that fishing at Blagdon is not limited to the loch-style. In June, hatches can justify switching to more traditional dry-fly sight-fishing techniques.)

Competitions are part of the tradition on English stillwater fisheries, and Blagdon is not an exception. Anglers compete for modest prizes, and immodest bragging rights. "Most reservoirs have a tourney or two each season," Perk explained. "I usually go great lengths to avoid such things, but I made an exception at Blagdon. The events are cere-moniously conducted and provide a bit of insight into English culture. Being able to par-take in a tourney was a nice complement to the overall Blagdon experience."

PERK PERKINS has led Orvis as president and CEO since November 1992. He came to work for Orvis in 1977 and has held many positions in the company. Perk is an avid and accomplished fly fisherman, wing shooter, canoeist, cross-country skier, and bird watch-er. He dedicates considerable energy to conservation issues, and serves as vice chairman of the Nature Conservancy. He has led the company's support of conservation (5 percent of pretax profits) with the mantra, "If we are going to benefit from our natural resources, we must be willing to take action to protect them."

IF YOU GO

▶ **Prime Time:** Blagdon Lake is open to fishing from late March to late November. The lake fishes well most of the season (especially when it's windy.), though fishing slows down somewhat in the dog days of summer – mid-July through August.

▶ **Getting There:** Blagdon Lake is approximately 120 miles from London. While rail service can get you close, the best way to reach the region is by car.

▶ **Accommodations:** A number of lodging options – bed and breakfasts, inns, and hotels – are available in and around Blagdon. Visit www.ukvillages.co.uk for a comprehensive listing. Of course, your real home away from home in England is the pub, and there are a dozen within three miles of Blagdon, including the White Lion, the Lamb and Flag Inn, the Queens Arms, the Holman Clavel Inn, and the White Hart Inn.

▶ **Equipment:** A 9-foot or 10-foot rod for 6- or 7-weight line is appropriate for Blagdon. The three-fly rig that Perk described is the most common rig on Blagdon, with tippet at the point being 6-pound test. Smaller nymphs are generally used; the tackle shop at Blagdon Lodge can set you up with the local favorites. Day and afternoon fishing permits are available from the Blagdon and Woodford Lodges. Sixteen rowboats are available for hire. Advance booking is advisable, especially on weekends. Prices for boat fishing are £21 per person; for bank fishing, £14 per person. For information, contact Bob Hanford at +44 1275 33 23 39, or visit www.bristolwater.co.uk/fishing/lakes.htm. With advance notice, the lodges can arrange a guide.

15
DESTINATION

BROWN TROUT ON THE
RIVER TEST

RECOMMENDED BY **Simon Gawesworth**

The chalkstreams of Hampshire in southern England hold a dear place in the world's collective fly-fishing soul. From the time of Izaak Walton and Piscator, Hampshire has been known for its "swift, shallow, clear, pleasant brooks, and store of Trouts." These nutrient-rich waters (chalkstreams are so named because their waters bubble up through chalk formations, neutralizing acidity and adding mineral content) have historically fostered vast legions of insect life, including many mayflies. It was amidst these carefully manicured riverbanks and idyllic meadows that many of the precepts of modern trout fishing were tested and, to a great degree, perfected. Through the center of it all flows the Test.

The Test bubbles up north of Hampshire in the town of Ashe. As it travels to the southwest, it is joined by the Bourne, then the Dever and the Anton. At thirty-nine miles, it is the longest of the Hampshire chalkstreams. Through much of its path, the Test is not one river but a collection of tributaries, feeder creeks, mill channels, and carriers (man-made sloughs created initially for irrigation). The Upper Test is small, shallow water, with a good concentration of wild brown trout. The Middle Test is similar in character to the Upper, though on a larger scale, with longer, deeper pools that hold larger trout. Here, planted rainbows and browns supplement the native brown stock. In the last four miles below the town of Romsey, the river is reduced to one channel. There are fewer resident trout in this stretch, though the Lower Test is visited by sea trout and the occasional salmon.

While the Test was recognized as a trout-rich river in the 1500s, it did not become an angling destination until the industrial revolution spawned a leisure class in the 1800s. Londonites snapped up country estates in Hampshire, and cultivated the rivers for their amusement. Riverkeepers were employed to maintain a proper gardenlike setting;

OPPOSITE:
Most fishing
on the River
Test is done
from shore.
Wading
is largely
forbidden.

DESTINATION

16

an earlier generation of riverkeepers was employed to clear the river of weeds to maintain water flows for the mills of a distant agricultural era. It was in the 1880s that Frederic Halford, along with George Selwyn Marryat and William Lunn, conducted pioneering entomological studies on the Middle Test at Stockbridge. Halford's musings, captured in *Floating Flies and How to Dress Them* (1886) and *Dry Fly Fishing in Theory and Practice* (1889), became the bedrock of modern dry-fly fishing.

Simon Gawesworth first fished the Test in 1980, and the river made a deep impression. "In my opinion, the Test lives up to its great reputation," Simon confirmed. "It's still one of the most beautiful rivers I've ever fished. I think it's wise not to build the fishing itself up too much, as many of the fish are stocked. One visits for the Englishness of it all. It's a legend, part of the cult of fishing." Like other chalkstreams and spring creeks, the great clarity and slow tempo of the Test make it ideal for fishing dry flies. On many beats, fishing anything *but* dry flies is verboten. Other rules apply: one may cast only to feeding fish that have been sighted; one must cast upstream, and the fly cannot be fished below the angler; only one fly can be fished; and, on many beats, one may not wade into the river, so as not to stir up silt and weeds for anglers downstream. Some beats include small platforms over the river to facilitate casting. And, needless to say, one must reserve a rod for the privilege of fishing the Test.

The best time to be on the Test is the two- to three-week period in late May and early June when the river's greatest mayfly hatches occur. This period has been dubbed the "Duffer's Holiday," presumably because even the most casual angler could find success at this time due to the reckless trout behavior brought on by the profusion of insects. Green Drakes are the great focus at this time. The river also sees hatches of March Browns, Pale Morning Duns, and Blue-Winged Olives. Mayfly hatches have suffered in recent years, causing some alarm among local anglers. It's uncertain whether insects are suffering due to contaminants in the water or a decrease in weed habitat as a result of an overabundance of swans.

The carriers of the Test hold great appeal for Simon because of the intimacy they afford. "I especially like the beats around Whitchurch, on the upper river. There are lots of little carriers in that stretch. There was one in particular that I don't believe had ever been fished. It was higgledy-piggledy – completely overgrown with thistles and the like. I managed to find a sluicy little pool where I could cast a fly. It was only five feet wide. There was a big trout lying in the neck of the pool. It took me five casts to get a fly in there, but when I did, the fish took. It was a fine wild brown of two and a half pounds."

One piece of River Test angling lore that you are very unlikely to experience is the Houghton Club, the most exclusive fly-fishing assembly in the world. The club was founded in 1822 with thirteen members. Current membership has ballooned to twenty-five. Houghtonites control fishing rights on a good part of the middle river around Stockbridge. Little is known about the goings-on at the club, except that there is a changing area reserved for Prince Charles, should he decide to try his luck. The Houghton Club environs are off limits for commoners, but you can seek solace at the bar of the Grosvenor Hotel, where club proceedings are conducted, or perhaps at the pub at the Mayfly Inn, where feeding trout can be viewed from the beer garden.

SIMON GAWESWORTH is an international fly-casting champion. He has worked around the fly-fishing industry all his adult life, as an instructor and a consultant. He is a three-time winner of the South West Federation River Championships and has been a member of the English International team in the European and World Fly Fishing Championships; he recently served as captain and team manager. He is currently vice president of public relations and educational services for Rio Products.

IF YOU GO

▶ **Prime Time:** Duffer's Fortnight – the two to three weeks of the mayfly hatch in late May and early June – is considered the premium time on the river.
▶ **Getting There:** The chalkstream region of Hampshire is just seventy-five miles southwest of London, and less than an hour from Heathrow and Gatwick airports. There is train service to Winchester, which is a short cab ride to Stockbridge.
▶ **Accommodations:** There are several nice inns in Stockbridge, including the White Hart Inn (+44 1264 81 06 63) and the Grosvenor Hotel (+44 1264 81 06 06), home to the Houghton Club. Be sure to grab a pint at the Mayfly Inn (+44 1264 86 02 83). A "Heritage Fly Fishing Tour" focusing on the history of angling in Hampshire while providing opportunities to fish some of the chalkstreams is available from Fishing Breaks of London (+44 2073 59 88 18; www.fishingbreaks.co.uk). Four-day tours (with three days of fishing and accommodations) begin at £1,865.
▶ **Equipment:** An 8-foot or 9-foot, 4- or 5-weight rod with floating line in weight forward

or double taper will suffice for the Test. For terminal tackle, bring 9-foot leaders tapered to 3x–6x, and tippet in 4x, 5x, and 6x. Many mayfly patterns from home (Pale Morning Duns, Blue-Winged Olives, Adams) will work; the Orvis shop at Stockbridge (+44 1264 81 00 17) can help you select the appropriate flies for the day. Orvis (www.orvis.co.uk) also lets the famous Kimbridge (aka Ginger Beer) beat, as well as Timsbury 5 and Timsbury 6. Prices for shared beats are about £150; for more information, contact Judith Thornton at +44 1264 34 95 19 (thorntonj@orvis.co.uk).

PERMIT OFF THE FLORIDA KEYS

RECOMMENDED BY **Sandy Moret**

The waters around Islamorada in the Florida Keys have long been renowned for producing world-record bonefish and three-figure tarpon. They also provide an ideal habitat for permit – though until a few decades ago no one thought you could actually catch them on a fly with any regularity. Sandy Moret, along with a few other pioneers, set out to prove the doubters wrong.

"I came to South Florida in the early seventies," Sandy recalled. "Saltwater fly fishing was just beginning to become popular. I met Flip Pallot [host of ESPN's popular *Walker's Cay Chronicles*], who'd been raised there, and we started fishing together. We concentrated on tarpon, redfish, and bonefish. There weren't many permit that had been caught on a fly at this point. You'd see them when you were bonefishing – they'd be on the same flats, out a bit deeper. We'd catch one here and there, but there was no method to it. Then about 1980, Del Brown started focusing on permit, with Steve Huff as his guide. Others followed. We figured that if we worked at it, someone could come up with a fly and a way to catch them."

Sandy and a few cohorts started innovating with different flies. "One was a shrimp-like pattern tied with chenille – the Puff – that Captain Nat Ragland came up with. Using that, the guys would get a permit every four or five trips. Then Steve Huff and Harry Spear began experimenting with epoxy. They came up with a fly they called the Mo – it was diamond-shaped, and looked like a crab. This was a fly that gave anglers a decent chance to catch a permit."

Over the years, it's safe to say that Sandy Moret has come up with a way to catch them. In July 2003, he caught his one-hundredth permit, multiples more than most hard-core saltwater anglers can ever hope to catch. His co-conspirator, Del Brown, landed more

than five hundred before his death in June 2003. (There is a namesake tournament held each March in the Keys to honor the accomplishments of this extraordinary angler.) If you've ever seen a fishing-magazine photo of a bearded fellow holding a permit by the tail with his mouth spread open in a howl, odds are that it is Sandy.

Most anglers agree that permit – *Trachinotus falcatus* – are salt water's holy grail. A cousin of the more plentiful pompano, it's blunt face, broad body, large round eyes, and scythelike tail make it readily recognizable. The permit's unique aerodynamics lend it a physical prowess that is unrivaled (in many an angler's view) by any other species; they've been known to take 150 yards of backing out in their first run! Secretive, antsy, and ever-alert, permit are also the spookiest creatures on the flats. In his definitive title *Bonefishing!*, Randall Kaufmann states, "If any fish can steal the limelight from bonefish, it's permit."

For Sandy Moret, it is both the permit's power and its peckishness that make it a prime target. "They're very strong fish and have very keen eyesight. They run hard, and if they get out in the current they can dog you forever. You have to do a lot of things right to get them to bite. It's a great challenge."

The Florida Keys seem as if they were created by central casting in response to a call for a saltwater fly-fishing wonderland. The numerous estuaries feeding the Florida Bay combined with the proximity of the Gulf Stream and myriad flats create a marine environment where water is ever in flux. Constantly circulating water, ample cover, and proximity to deeper water support a tremendous amount of bait, which in turn sustains tremendous game-fish populations, despite heavy fishing pressure.

"On the Keys, you can follow the tides up and down and catch incoming and outgoing flows at different spots," Sandy said. "You can always find a good tide, and this really extends the fishing day. You might travel a hundred miles in a day chasing those tides, but it's usually worthwhile." Permit generally prefer deeper water but will come into the flats on the incoming tide to feed. Larger fish usually travel alone or in pairs, but smaller fish can be seen in schools of ten to twenty fish. While permit will eat shrimp and baitfish, they love crabs. The evolution of good crab patterns has done a lot to bridge the gap between fishing for permit and catching permit. "With the flies we have today, the right conditions, and a permit focus, a decent angler has a decent chance to hook up."

What does it take to hook up? Sandy shared some of his secrets: "First, you need to go with the right guides who have a strong understanding of the tides and where the fish

OPPOSITE:
Photographer
R. Valentine
Atkinson poses
with a hard-
won permit.

17

DESTINATION

are going to be on a given tide. Second, you need a bright, sunny day. A springtime day when it's not too hot, a couple days after a cold front's come through, is ideal. After the front has passed, you have superbright blue skies. A strong tide – either new moon or full moon – is nice. When the tides are fast, fish have to make a fast decision on whether to eat a fly or not, and this is definitely in the angler's favor. Next, you want some wind; fifteen miles per hour is perfect, as this will put a little ripple on the surface and make it tougher for the fish to spot you. Finally, the angler needs to be able to cast forty or fifty feet into that fifteen-mile-per-hour wind, with a heavy fly. Crabs live on the bottom, and you need a fly with some lead eyes to get down fast."

The sight of a permit's unmistakable tail swathing the air as it roots for crustaceans on the flats is a dream come true for every angler who's ever hoped to land one of these great sport fish. Take a deep breath, make the cast, let the fly sink, twitch it ever so slightly when it reaches the bottom, say a prayer that the fish will take it ... and then hold on.

SANDY MORET owns and operates the Florida Keys Fly Fishing School and Outfitters; the school brings together some of the biggest names in saltwater fly fishing. Sandy is a nine-time Grand Champion of the Keys' most prestigious fly-fishing tournaments, has been a guest angler on the *Walker's Cay Chronicles* and *The Reel Guys* television programs, and has fished and explored throughout the Bahamas, Central America, and Palau. He helped pioneer Russian Atlantic salmon fishing on the Ponoi and has held many elected and appointed positions in regard to Everglades restoration.

IF YOU GO

▶ **Prime Time:** Spring and fall tend to be best, though permit are present throughout the year. Weather conditions (as described above) can make a summer or winter day equally attractive.

▶ **Getting There:** The Florida Keys begin at Upper Key Largo, roughly sixty miles from Miami, and extend just over one hundred miles to Key West. Islamorada, which is located at mile marker 82, makes a good base. In addition to proximity to permit, the waters off Islamorada host some of the best tarpon and bonefishing available anywhere.

▶ **Accommodations:** Islamorada has a range of lodging options, from the more upscale Cheeca Lodge (888-367-7625) to the more budget-conscious Days Inn (305-664-3681).

▶ **Equipment:** A 9-foot rod in 9- or 10-weight is recommended. Bring both a floating line and a slow-sinking line, and be sure you have a minimum of 200 yards of backing. A 9-foot to 12-foot tapered leader in sizes ranging from 12- to 16-pound will suffice. Any number of crab patterns will work, including the Del Brown Permit Crab, Anderson McCrab, Fuzzy Merkin, and Puff; all flies should be tied on #1/0 to #3/0 hooks. Permit fishing is extremely challenging so you'll need a guide (don't feel bad – even the late Del Brown, who caught more permit than anyone will likely ever catch, relied on guide Steve Huff). Through its fly-fishing school, Florida Keys Outfitters (305-664-5423; www.florida keysoutfitters.com) is plugged in to some of the very best saltwater fly-fishing guides in the world. Be very specific that you want to focus on permit. If you happen to get a permit early enough in the day, you may want to go for the Grand Slam of a permit, tarpon, and bonefish in a single day.

17

DESTINATION

ATLANTIC SALMON ON THE

LAXA I ADALDAL

RECOMMENDED BY **Mike Fitzgerald, Sr.** AND **Mike Fitzgerald, Jr.**

Sometimes, Norway's loss is the world's gain. At least that was the case for Atlantic salmon fishing aficionados, as Mike Fitzgerald, Sr., tells the story. "In the late sixties, I was introduced to a travel agent in New York who represented a Norwegian company that did booking for some of the famous salmon rivers – the Alta and the Laerdal among them – as well as other Norwegian adventures. Working with this fellow was my entrée into the Atlantic salmon travel business. In the early seventies, the Norwegian fishery showed some decline, thanks to drift netting and other issues. The Norwegian travel outfit figured they'd better diversify to please their salmon-fishing customers, and Iceland was appealing."

Mike Sr. had heard some good things about the fishing there, especially Laxa i Adaldal, which many simply call the Big Laxa. Ernie Schwiebert and Lee and Joan Wulff had fished there, and he'd seen Bing Crosby fishing there on *American Sportsman*. Mike Sr. took his first trip over in 1972 with a Texan named Wally Tabor. In four days, they landed sixteen fish between them, all between 12 and 20 pounds. "It was a wonderful first impression," Mike recalled. "We knew little about fishing the river, so we figured that if we could have success, then anyone could."

This is not to say that fishing on the Big Laxa is easy. Originating at Lake Myvatn in northern Iceland and fed by numerous springs, the river has the clarity and complex currents of a spring creek. Weed growth, encouraged by high alkalinity, furthers the spring-creek metaphor. Sight-fishing opportunities are rare here, as the salmon blend in with the packed lava sand bottom. If one is fortunate enough to hook a fish, aforementioned weeds and sharp lava bedrock stand at the ready to relieve you of your quarry. "The tradition on the Big Laxa is to use small flies on double hooks," Mike Sr. said. "The stan-

OPPOSITE:
Some good
pools on the
Big Laxa are
best fished
from a boat.

dard is size six, and many fish are taken on size eights and tens. For me, catching large fish on small flies intensifies the sport. It's almost all floating-line fishing on the Laxa. Fish respond well to riffle-hitched flies, which they'll take on the swing. For some reason, these fish are reluctant to take dry flies, though they'll return to a wet fly again and again before taking. On one occasion, I had a fish move for the fly eighteen or twenty times before it finally took."

Most of the pools on the Laxa can be fished by wading or from shore, though a few are fished from a boat using the classic drop-down method. It depends on the angler's inclination. "A nice thing about the Laxa is that older people or people with infirmities can access the river easily," Mike Sr. added. "Beats are close to the lodge, no more than fifteen minutes, and every angler has plenty of elbow room." Relative to many Atlantic salmon fisheries, the Big Laxa is fairly close – four and a half hours from the eastern United States to Reykjavik, and another forty-five-minute flight up to Husavik. One can conceivably take a red-eye flight on Saturday night and be fishing Sunday afternoon. Many visitors value the Laxa because conditions are reliable. Variances in water levels are minimal and the water temperatures are very consistent.

Befitting its nickname, the Laxa i Adaldal is one of Iceland's largest salmon rivers, and it consistently produces the nation's heaviest fish. "Large" in Iceland has traditionally meant fish of greater than 20 pounds, though there is evidence that suggests this may be changing. According to noted salmon angler and author Art Lee, fish in the 40-pound class have recently been hooked (though not landed). The incidence of larger fish returning to the Big Laxa is credited to catch-and-release fishing practiced on some beats of the river. Large or not, most anglers feel that Laxa salmon can hold their own with fish from any system. "I'd put an eighteen-pound Laxa fish up against an eighteen-pound salmon anywhere," said Mike Fitzgerald, Jr., who first joined his dad in Iceland at the tender age of twelve ... and promptly caught three fish in the first hour of his first trip. "I've fished just about everywhere for Atlantic salmon, and the Big Laxa fish seem hotter to me. I'll have a fish on and the line will be pointing downstream, and the fish will be jumping eighty yards upstream. They are incredibly strong, and incredible jumpers."

Northern Iceland provides a dramatic backdrop for the pursuit of *Salmo salar*. The dense stands of pines and hardwoods that anglers often equate with Atlantic salmon waters are replaced by vast open valleys, bracketed by snowcapped mountains that rise to the west and north. "It's more reminiscent of Tierra del Fuego or northern Alaska, with no trees, a couple of camps, and very few roads," Mike Jr. added. "The Icelanders have two sayings about trees. One goes, 'There is a naked woman behind every tree in Iceland.' The other is, 'If you ever get lost in the Icelandic National Forest, all you have to do is stand up.'"

It's a bit of a tradition to take a nip of something each time a fish is landed. As drinking is not an unpopular pastime in Iceland, the guides are happy to help. "The guides we work with are great fun to be on the stream with. They're companions, and they enjoy the fishermen. Their toast of choice is a potion called Brenevin. It's a cousin of Aquavit. Icelanders call it Black Death. One nip is usually enough for non-Icelanders." There are no reports of anglers breaking off fish to avoid their dose of Black Death.

MIKE FITZGERALD, SR., founded Frontiers International Travel with his wife, Susie, in 1969 and has served as president and chief executive officer of the company for the past thirty-four years. He was involved in the early development of a number of fly-fishing destinations that remain mainline Frontiers programs today. These include flats fishing on Mexico's Yucatán Peninsula, Christmas Island, the Ponoi River in Russia, shooting and fishing in Argentina, and fishing in both Iceland and the Alta River in Norway. His travels have included fifty-three countries on five continents. He has served on various boards of directors, including the Atlantic Salmon Federation and the American Museum of Fly Fishing.

MIKE FITZGERALD, JR., graduated from Duke University in 1987 with a degree in sociology and economics at which time he joined Frontiers full time. Over the years, Mike has handled a number of different fly-fishing and bird-hunting programs for Frontiers. Today, as part of the senior management team and president-elect, Mike works most closely with the North America, South America, Saltwater, and South Pacific departments. He is also very involved with overall company marketing, supplier relations, and business development. Mike is on the board of the American Fly Fishing Trade Association and Friends of Turneffe Atoll in Belize.

18

DESTINATION

IF YOU GO

▶ **Prime Time:** The season runs from June 10 to September 10, but the Big Laxa hits its peak from mid-July to mid-August.

▶ **Getting There:** To reach the Big Laxa, you'll need to fly to Reykjavik, and then on to Husavik. Both are served by Iceland Air (800-223-5500; www.icelandair.com) and partner airline Air Iceland. Service to Reykjavik is available from Boston, New York, Baltimore/Washington, Orlando, and Minneapolis.

▶ **Accommodations:** The lodge at Laxa i Adaldal (booked through Frontiers International Travel, www.frontierstravel.com) is clean and comfortable, as you'd expect in this nation of Scandinavian roots. World-class chefs from Reykjavik cycle through the lodge as part of their "vacation," offering up some of the best lodge cuisine you'll find anywhere. The Steingrimsdottir family works hard to make guests feel at home. Space is limited to seven anglers; guests can expect to pay up to $6,500 during prime season.

▶ **Equipment:** The Big Laxa is fished with both 9-foot rods and spey rods; either should be in 8-weight. Rods should be outfitted with a floating line and ample backing. A 9-foot leader tapered to ox will work, with 8-, 10-, and 12-pound tippet. Small flies – generally #8s or #10s – tied on double hooks are most popular, and patterns that include blue are favored by Big Laxa veterans. Some favorites are the Laxa Blue, Blue Charm, Hairy Mary Gray, Bill Young, the Betsy, and the Sally; the latter three were developed by guide Petur Steingrimsson, who's recognized as one of Iceland's salmon gurus and was once featured wearing his trademark sweater in an advertisement for Sage fly rods.

Finally, please note that Icelandic authorities require a veterinarian's certificate stating that your tackle has been sterilized. A sample vet's letter will be supplied with pretrip information from your booking agent.

RAINBOW TROUT ON THE
HENRY'S FORK

RECOMMENDED BY **Lori-Ann Murphy**

Four years after Lewis and Clark had returned east from their little journey, a fur trader named Andrew Henry stumbled upon the river in what is now the state of Idaho that came to be known as Henry's Fork. Trout anglers the world over will do well to raise a toast to Major Henry, for he discovered what many consider to be America's greatest trout stream.

"I'd always heard about this area and the Henry's Fork," said Lori-Ann Murphy. "When I first visited, I said, 'I've got live here someday.' Eventually, I made the move. There's always something going on in terms of hatches on the river, and there's something for everyone – riffles, flat water, social fishing, and solitude fishing. The Henry's character is always changing. It keeps you on your toes."

Like most great rivers, the diversity of the Henry's Fork makes it seem like many fisheries. The common ingredients are the region's astounding natural beauty and opportunities to view wildlife that call Greater Yellowstone home. Henry's Lake, one source of the Henry's headwaters, has rainbow/cutthroat hybrids that can sometimes top 10 pounds and are capable of straightening large hooks; it's best fished from a float tube. Box Canyon, a stretch of four river miles below Island Park Reservoir, is fast and furious and not for the faint of heart, yet its runs and pockets of holding water yield some of Henry's largest rainbows, which will often fall prey to a big ugly nymph. (First-timers will do well to engage a guide for this section.)

Each section of the Henry's Fork has its special characteristics and tales of wonderful fish fooled and forsaken. If there's one section of river that engages the collective fly-fishing imagination, it probably would be the stretch that flows through Harriman State Park, known to some as the "Railroad Ranch" or simply "the Ranch."

At first glance, the waters of the Ranch seem a bit slow and unstructured to qualify as the ground zero of the fly fishers' Mecca. A closer look – and better yet a cast – will illustrate the myriad currents that exist, seemingly to frustrate the drifts of anglers desperately casting to feeding fish. Dense weed beds cover much of the bottom, providing a rich food source and cover for the fish, which are mostly rainbows. There are many smaller fish here but also a good population of trout in the 20-inch range. These are sophisticated fish that have seen a few fishermen. Sloppy presentations and wading will put them down fast. (Many Henry's regulars prefer to sight-fish for their quarry, limiting the often pointless flailing that discourages fish from rising if a hatch does occur.)

Prolific insect hatches – hatches that might occur simultaneously – have earned the Ranch much of its acclaim. Western Green Drakes, Pale Morning Duns, Brown Drakes, Gray Drakes, Mahogany Duns, and Blue-Winged Olives all make an appearance here. (There's also a huge salmonfly hatch, though it generally trails off by the time the Ranch opens for fishing.)

When a hatch does come off, fish respond eagerly. You might find half a dozen or a dozen fish feeding within casting range. Seasoned Henry's anglers offer two bits of advice: 1) choose one feeding fish and focus your efforts on that fish, and 2) present your fly downstream or across to the fish you choose to focus on. This last tip might seem anathema to fly anglers schooled in the "dry-fly upstream" methodology, but there's a reason. As alluded to above, your fly won't likely be the first that these fish have seen. If at all possible, you want the fish to see your offering *before* it sees your tippet/leader. Under the spring-creek like circumstances of the Ranch, this is best achieved with a down or down-and-across presentation.

Many are attracted to fly fishing because they perceive it as an individualist hobby that presents an opportunity to enjoy solitude. The sport, however, does have its social occasions. One of the most notable is the opening of the Ranch section of the Henry's on June 15. This opening date stems from an agreement between the Harriman family (who donated the land in 1977) and the state of Idaho. The Harrimans wanted the land managed harmoniously for man and wildlife, which means they didn't want hundreds of anglers tramping through the nesting grounds of the birds who call this area home. When the birds leave, the anglers can come in.

Lori-Ann Murphy almost always makes it to the opening of the Ranch. "It's a huge rendezvous, and a magical time to be on the river. People who've been seeing each other

OPPOSITE:
A lone angler
awaits the
hatch on
the Ranch
section of
Henry's Fork.

DESTINATION **19**

91

for twenty to twenty-five years show up. It may be the only time they see each other in a given year. I've never fished the Test or Itchen in England, but I imagine it's like that. There's tremendous camaraderie. Some seasons are more prolific with bug life than others, but no one cares too much. There's a lot of love around this gathering, and this place. There are a lot of familiar faces and a lot of famous fly-fishing faces, but it's not stuffy. Newcomers are welcome, so long as they behave with some decorum – and don't walk between an angler and the fish he's trying to raise. If you show bad etiquette out on the river, you'll be crucified."

LORI-ANN MURPHY moved from Seattle to the Jackson, Wyoming, region in 1988, at least in part to be close to the fishing she loved. She soon left the health care profession and founded Reel Women Outfitters in Victor, Idaho. Lori-Ann has many years of experience as a professional fly-fishing guide on her favorite rivers in Idaho, Wyoming, and Montana. She worked as the fly-fishing consultant for Meryl Streep and Kevin Bacon in the movie *The River Wild*. As an adviser for the Orvis Company, she can be found in the off season giving presentations at sports shows and banquets.

IF YOU GO

▶ **Prime Time:** The upper section of Henry's Fork (discussed here) is open from late May to November, with the exception of Harriman State Park, which opens in the middle of June, just in time for the famed Green Drake hatch. Fishing is good through the season; some anglers feel that the Henry's is best in the fall – plus, there are fewer people.

▶ **Getting There:** Last Chance, Idaho, is approximately forty miles south of West Yellowstone, and sixty miles north of Idaho Falls, which is served by Delta, Sky West, and Horizon. It is a four-and-a-half-hour drive from Salt Lake City.

▶ **Accommodations:** There are several options in the greater Last Chance, Idaho, region. Last Chance Lodge (800-428-8338; www.hydeoutfitters.com) offers room-and-meal packages from $105 per night, and two-day/three-night guided packages for about $690 per person (both based on double occupancy). Angler's Lodge (208-558-9555; www.anglerslodge.net) in Island Park offers rooms from $59 to $159. For a more upscale stay, there's Henry's Fork Lodge (208-558-7953; www.henrysforklodge.com), which offers rooms from $300 per person, based on double occupancy. There are campgrounds, too.

▶ **Equipment:** A 9-foot 5- or 6-weight rod outfitted with a floating line will handle most situations on Henry's Fork, while 9- to 12-foot leaders tapered to 5x will give you enough muscle to land larger rainbows; bring tippet in 2- to 6-pound test. The complex hatches of the Henry's Fork preclude a comprehensive list of fly patterns, but a few prominent hatches you may encounter, depending on when you visit, include: salmonflies, Pale Morning Duns, Blue-Winged Olives, Green Drakes, Brown Drakes, caddis, Tricos, Callibaetis, and Mahogany Duns. Some terrestrials are also encountered. Henry's Fork Anglers (800-788-4479, www.henrysforkanglers.com) is on the banks of the river at Last Chance. The shop's owner, Mike Lawson, is considered by many to be the authority on the river, and the shop can help you unravel the hatches. They also provide guide services. Lori-Ann Murphy's company, Reel Women (208-787-2657, www.reel-women.com) also guides on the Henry's.

19

DESTINATION

CUTTHROAT TROUT ON THE MIDDLE FORK OF THE SALMON RIVER

RECOMMENDED BY **Bryce Tedford**

On a June day in 1805 near Great Falls, Montana, Meriwether Lewis recorded the Corps of Discovery's first encounter with a cutthroat trout:

> These trout are from sixteen to twenty three inches in length, precisely resemble our moun-
> tain or speckled trout in form and the position of their fins, but the specks on these are of a
> deep black instead of the red or goald colour of those common in the U.' States. These are
> furnished long sharp teeth on the pallet and tongue and have generally a small dash of red
> on each side behind the front ventral fins; the flesh is of a pale yellowish red, or when in good
> order, of a rose red.
>
> —Meriwether Lewis, *The Journals of Lewis and Clark*

Cutthroat trout hold a warm spot in the hearts of anglers. They are a beautiful fish, as Lewis described. And they are a very willing fish. A valid scientific study showed cutthroat the easiest trout to catch by angling methods, followed in difficulty by brook, rainbow, and brown trout.

Progress has not been kind to the cutthroat. Today's distribution is a fraction of what it once was, and two of its subspecies are extinct. Extremely sensitive to changes in water quality, cutts have been hurt by stream degradation brought on by logging and livestock grazing. They've also been harmed by the introduction of nonnative trout species. The Middle Fork of the Salmon – framed by the Sawtooth and Salmon River Mountains in the heart of the Frank Church–River of No Return Wilderness in central Idaho – remains a stronghold for native west-slope cutthroat. Anglers could hardly hope for a prettier place to pursue this most becoming salmonid. Bryce Tedford agrees.

OPPOSITE:
An angler
works one of
the clear creeks
that feed the
Middle Fork.

DESTINATION 20

95

"There are few if any other rivers in the lower forty-eight where you can float a hundred miles of pristine, roadless wilderness, with ever-changing terrain, and cast to free-rising cutthroat trout through the whole trip. The fish are opportunistic, as the Middle Fork isn't especially rich in food. They're willing to take flies on top all day long, whether there's a hatch on or not."

Fishing is not complicated on the Middle Fork. A larger attractor pattern like a Stimulator, Schroeder's Hopper, or Parachute Adams in size 10, dead-drifted against a granite wall, behind a midriver rock, or a back eddy, will often bring a rise. Surface action can become especially vigorous in early July, when hatches of salmonflies and golden stones are prolific. Cutts here are not particularly large (they average 12 inches to 14 inches, with the occasional fish to 20 inches), but they are plentiful enough to provide steady action throughout the day. An angler with modest skills can expect to hook thirty to fifty fish a day during the high season. The cutts' cooperative nature is one of the Middle Fork's charms.

"We have quite a few families on the river, because there's something for everyone," Bryce explained. "The anglers in the family can take a drift boat and fish all day, while other family members can raft and hike and swim. As a guide, it's really wonderful taking a father and child duo out on the river, where the child can't really cast yet. On day one, we focus on teaching the rudiments of casting. By day two, I can sit back and watch the child make the cast, set the hook, and play the fish in. Being able to watch the father watch his child get his or her first fish is just fantastic. Another thing I really enjoy about the Middle Fork is the clarity of the water. You can spot a fish, cast to it, and watch it come up and roll on the fly. The whole process unfolds before your eyes."

On a Middle Fork trip, the path is the goal. The scenery is spectacular; at the Boundary Creek put-in the river is small and fast, hemmed in closely by thick forests of Douglas fir and spruce. As you proceed downriver, the canyon opens up to expose jaw-dropping crags of Idaho batholith. Bighorn sheep and mountain goat practice their acrobatic routines here. Several natural hot springs present themselves along the river's 106-mile course; Sunflower Showers, a hot spring that includes natural pools and a makeshift shower, is especially nurturing for sore casting shoulders. You can also hike into the canyon at certain points to view Native American pictographs and pioneer homesteads. Oh yes, there's also a bit of white water on the river. Most rafting enthusiasts place the Middle Fork in the top ten white-water rivers of the world.

On a typical float day, a hearty breakfast is served at seven-thirty. You'll be on the river fishing by nine, and in the coming evening's camp by five, ready for a cocktail or two followed by a steak, pork chop, or salmon dinner. Nearly all the fishing on the Middle Fork is done from a drift boat, though several feeder streams along the course of the trip provide anglers with an opportunity to walk and wade on their own. The pocket water Loon, Camas, and Big Creeks offer is a pleasant contrast to the bigger water, and the same attractor patterns yield good results for redband trout and cutthroats. Gray wolves were reintroduced to the Frank Church area several years ago, and in the upper stretches of the river their howls can be heard in the evening. There's perhaps no better sound to punctuate the western wilderness trout-fishing experience the Middle Fork affords.

BRYCE TEDFORD began guiding fly fishers around his native Puget Sound when he was eighteen. Since that time, he has guided steelheaders on the Deschutes, John Day, and Grande Ronde rivers in Oregon, and trout anglers on the rivers of Patagonia and the Middle Fork. His fishing adventures have taken him throughout the Pacific Northwest.

IF YOU GO

▶ **Prime Time:** Flow and weather conditions are ideal in July, though the river generally fishes well from June through September.

▶ **Getting There:** Middle Fork floats begin with a bush-plane flight from Boise to a put-in site on the river. Salmon Air (800-448-3413) is a reliable air taxi service that can spir-it you to any number of remote airstrips along the river corridor for about $125. The only other way in is by horseback, or hiking trail.

▶ **Accommodations:** While a number of outfitters run white-water-oriented trips on the Middle Fork, Solitude River Trips (800-396-1776; www.rivertrips.com) focuses on fly fishing. They run the Middle Fork in drift boats (which facilitates casting) and are Dutch-oven wizards come mealtime. The rate for a six-day/five-night wilderness float is $2,500.

▶ **Equipment:** A 9-foot 5-weight rod outfitted with a floating line will accommodate all situations on the Middle Fork. 9-foot leaders tapered to 4x, with tippet material in 4x and 5x, will be fine. Standby flies: Elk Hair Caddis Light & Dark (#10-#14); Schroeder's Parachute Hopper (#10-#12); Royal Wulff (#10-#14); Parachute Adams (#10-#14); Stimulators in orange, yellow, and green (#8-#12); and Royal Trudes (#10-#14).

GIANT TREVALLY OFF
CHRISTMAS ISLAND

RECOMMENDED BY **Lance** AND **Randall Kaufmann**

Christmas Island is an isolated coral atoll some 1,200 miles south of Honolulu. The first European discovery of the island came on Christmas Eve of 1777, courtesy of Captain James Cook. The island was viewed as a good source of turtle meat, but was otherwise forgotten. Christmas Island's second great discovery came during World War II, when it was established as a staging area for Allied troops heading to the Pacific; in the Cold War era, Christmas Island served as a testing ground for nuclear weapons. The most recent conquest of the island has been gentler, and a greater source of joy. In the early 1980s, Christmas Island was opened for sportfishing. Since that time, it has become renowned as one of the world's most prolific and reliable bonefishing venues. "When Christmas Island started, we came for the bonefishing," Randall Kaufmann recalled. "But when we started fishing for giant trevally, we began to forget about the bonefish."

Giant trevally (*Caranx ignobilis*) are the largest of the thirty-three species of trevally indigenous to the Pacific and Indian oceans. Trevally are the Pacific counterpart of the permit of the Atlantic, with one notable exception: they are extremely aggressive and thus much easier to catch. GTs are distinguished from other trevally by their steeper head profile and the absence of a dark spot on the rear of their gill covers. They are generally silver and can have golden highlights that hint of phosphorescence. GTs eat anything they can catch, and bonefish are a favorite prey. "Sometimes you'll hook a bonefish at Christmas, and it will scream toward the edge of the flats," Lance Kaufmann said. "Then, suddenly, it's racing back at you, even though you're in two feet of water. You can be sure that the bonefish on your line has seen a trevally." Giant trevally around Christmas Island reach giant proportions. Though fish average 15 to 30 pounds, GTs to 50 pounds are often hooked by fly fishers, and mammoths of over 100 pounds are sometimes

OPPOSITE:
The hard
sand flats of
Christmas
Island make
for ideal
wading.

encountered. "The GTs are so big, you can see them coming from far off," Lance continued. "You'll see a head, then a fin, then an eye. At times, they're moving so fast, they're like a mirage." By all reports, visitors won't soon forget the sight of a 30-pound trevally screaming through the shallows with half of its body above the surface of the water.

"Sometimes the trevally will gather in small gangs – three, four, or five fish in a group," Randall continued. "They remind me of street gangs. In the groups, there are one or two muscle fish, the leaders of the pack. They attack whatever they can get. Those are the fish you want to target."

GTs are often encountered while bonefishing. If you're on the flats, it's a good idea to have an 11- or 12-weight rod loaded and ready to go. (If you retain a personal guide, he can carry your trevally rod as you fish for bones. He'll also help you spot more fish.) Trevally will often cruise the edge of a flat along the drop-off, looking for action. They'll dart into the flats when see they some prey. If you're wading a flat and spot a GT on the move, grab the big rod, lead the fish with a cast quite a bit in front of it, and strip like crazy. They like poppers, and the takes can be almost scary. "They'll follow the popper for a few feet and then explode," Lance explained. "When they take, there's a hole in the water six feet wide and a foot and a half deep."

Lance related a story that speaks to the kind of intimidation GTs can provoke. "We were working a flat and saw two large objects out near the reef. Were they rocks? No! They were two GTs, they were at least a hundred pounds each, and they were coming right at us. I flipped the fly in their general direction as they bore down. The leader wasn't beyond the eye of the rod when one fish took the fly. The other one swam right between me and the guide. It was scary. Meanwhile, the fish that took the fly just went and went and went. He cleaned me out, three hundred yards of backing, fly line, everything!" Some anglers keying on GTs will fish from a skiff, searching out the fish near the drop-offs, or ambushing them as they cut across the flat. Battles with GTs in the 30-pound class and larger can last half an hour or more. Be prepared!

When you need to give your heart a rest from the marauding antics of GTs, rumor has it that the bonefishing on Christmas Island isn't bad. The island's main lagoon is a labyrinth of flats interwoven with channels. Some flats will contain vast schools of smaller fish in the 2- to 5-pound range; others will hold a few large cruisers in the 10-pound class, or even larger. The flats are firm and can be easily waded, and white sand bottoms make it easier for tyros to spot fish. Wind is seldom an issue. "Christmas Island is a great

DESTINATION 21

spot for a first-time flats fisher," Randall said. "It's not very technical, and the fish are always present." On a good day, a competent angler can expect to tangle with fifteen to twenty bones, sometimes more. If you're focusing on bonefish, you'll likely get a couple shots a day at giant trevally. If you're targeting GTs and using a skiff, you may have ten to fifteen opportunities.

Christmas Island is a unique place, but don't expect a tropical paradise. There's no lush vegetation here, and on a walk about the island you may encounter detritus from the bomb testing-ground days (though there are no traces of radiation) and other flotsam of the military-industrial complex's whims. Still, the island is home to exotic bird life, including sooty terns, frigatebirds, and boobies. There is also first-class diving around the reef that can bring you in close contact with tremendous coral formations and, potentially, some of your prey. "If you go out to the mouth of the lagoon when the tide is going out," Randall said, "you'll see a hundred trevally milling around, waiting for whatever might get flushed out."

LANCE KAUFMANN is co-owner of Kaufmann's Streamborn, Inc., a retail and mail-order fly-fishing supply company with stores in Portland, Oregon, and Seattle and Bellevue, Washington, and Kaufmann's Fly Fishing Expeditions, Inc., which outfits anglers headed to exotic destinations. Lance has visited many of the world's famous fishing destinations and has been outfitting anglers for thirty years. He has specialized in Christmas Island trevally since the mid-1980s.

RANDALL KAUFMANN is a renowned expert on fly fishing and flies and is the author of several books on the subject, including *Tying Dry Flies* and *Tying Nymphs*. His book *Bonefishing!* is considered one of the definitive works on saltwater fly fishing. Randall has traveled extensively with fly rod, camera, and pen and explored many of the world's "secret" spots while they were still secret.

IF YOU GO

▶ **Prime Time:** Any time you can go! Being so close to the equator, Christmas Island has extremely consistent weather, and fishes well each week of the year.

▶ **Getting There:** Package destinations to Christmas Island begin in Honolulu. From here a charter plane will spirit you to Kiribati; flights to and from the island depart on

Mondays. Package fees include charter airfare to Christmas Island. You should arrive in Honolulu at least a day before your departure for Kiribati.

▶ **Accommodations:** The most popular fly-fishing package on Christmas Island includes lodging at the Captain Cook Hotel, which offers oceanside bungalows and standard-issue motel rooms; the latter have air-conditioning. Digs here are not fancy but the showers are hot, the rooms are clean, and the food, which is served family style in a common room, is quite decent. Weeklong packages, which include lodging, meals, four guided days of skiff fishing in the lagoon, and two and a half days of roadside truck fishing, are $2,750. Christmas Island Outfitters have a smaller operation on the island as well.

▶ **Equipment:** For giant trevally, a 9-foot 11- or 12-weight rod is in order. Bring floating tropical line and clear intermediate sinking line, with at least 300 yards of backing; if you're chasing GTs offshore, a bigger rod with 400 yards of backing is needed. A 9-foot leader in 15- to 20-pound test outfitted with monofilament shock tippets in 50- to 80-pound test should suffice. As far as flies go, GTs are not too picky. Big poppers, Sea Habit Bucktails, and Deceivers in blue/white, red/yellow, and chartreuse/green, in #2/0 through #2 will work. For bonefish, pack a 9-foot 8-weight rod with floating tropical line and clear intermediate lines loaded with 200 yards of backing. Bring 9-foot bonefish leaders with tippet in 8- to 12-pound test. For flies, Christmas Island Specials (in pearlescent, pink/white, and chartreuse/white), Marabou Shrimp (in tan, pink, yellow, and white), and assorted crab patterns work well.

BROOK TROUT ON
THE WOODS RIVER SYSTEM

RECOMMENDED BY **James R. Babb**

When fly fishers first plied the waters of the New World in the 1700s, trout fishing meant *brook* trout fishing. Brookies (or squaretails or speckled trout) are the original trout of the East – though they're technically a member of the char family. Many a young boy cut his angling teeth catching hand-sized brookies from little creeks and ponds on worms or even strips of cloth, long before rainbow and German brown trout had gained a stronghold on the Eastern Seaboard.

Pretty and delicate as they are, forget about those little brookies for a moment, and consider the wilds of Labrador, a place where 10-plus-pound brook trout are a reality, and where James R. Babb and a few friends enjoyed a singularly perfect day of fishing.

"I had an invitation to go up to Labrador with a few friends – John Gierach and A. K. Best – to fish at a new wilderness outpost, Three Rivers Lodge," Jim remembered. "The first few days out of the lodge, we did pretty well, though nothing out of the ordinary for Labrador. On the third day, we flew into an outpost camp called Fifth Rapids. We came to some pocket water and noticed a small gray-winged dun coming off. A few fish were rising here and there. We all tied on some smallish dries and, in the next four or five hours, proceeded to catch upward of a hundred and fifty pounds of wild brook trout. I should add that we caught only about thirty fish. My smallest weighed about four pounds, my largest about seven. A.K. and John each got a fish around nine pounds, and I lost one fish that parted a fresh ten-pound leader between the knots. Later around the woodstove in the lodge, A.K. summed it up pretty well: 'That was the most outrageous day of fishing I've ever had.'"

Labrador is about as wild as things get in eastern North America. Three Rivers Lodge is a 150-mile floatplane flight from Labrador City, which isn't particularly close to anywhere. The thick spruce and tamarack forests here – home to black bear, bald eagle, and vast herds of migrating caribou – are bisected by the Woods River system, which includes nearly a hundred miles of river, lakes, and feeder streams. The lake sections hold trophy lake trout and northern pike; the big brookies concentrate in the stream sections that connect the lakes, especially in and below the riffles.

   The fishing here is not terrifically technical, yet the fish are not pushovers. "There are places up in the Arctic where you only need a pulse and a hook to catch fish," Jim said. "The fish at Fifth Rapids weren't pattern crazy, but the fly had to be presented right, with a dead drift. They were just skittish enough to make things fun without driving you crazy. In my opinion, big brook trout are much better fighters than other salmonids. They have to be extremely tough to survive in an environment where they're preyed upon by large pike. At one point, A.K. caught a two-pound brookie that was grabbed by a nine-pound pike before he could get it in. That's evolutionary theory borne out."

   One of the wonderful things about the Woods River system is the endless sense of fishing possibilities it presents. "There are probably spots equally as good as Fifth Rapids to fish," Jim said, "but they haven't been found yet. Only a quarter of the rivers up there have been explored by the guides at Three Rivers. If you and your guide are in an adventurous mood, you may have the chance to fish waters that have never been fished. I'm a big fan of little streams. There are hundreds of feeder creeks coming into the system. We stopped at one such creek that resembled a western irrigation ditch. On his first cast, John caught a six-pound brookie."

   Labrador is a brook trout nirvana, though it's a nirvana with a few drawbacks. The weather can be capricious; some days the rain and wind can be severe enough to keep even the hardiest anglers huddled around the stove. Additionally, the mosquitoes and blackflies can be more predatory than the pike, making heavy-duty bug spray and head nets a must. (During Jim's trip, a light wind kept the bugs mostly at bay, adding to the pleasure.) For the trophy brook trout enthusiast in search of a true wilderness experience, the chance of a washed-out day and a few mosquito bites will not be enough to deter a trip that harkens back to angling legend Lee Wulff's adventurous days in this part of the world. "The lodge has an old red Beaver floatplane, a real classic," Jim added. "For me, there are few things more fun than flying into a river that can't be fished any other way. It's just you, your buddies, and the fish."

JAMES R. BABB is angling editor of *Gray's Sporting Journal* and author of *Crosscurrents: A Flyfisher's Progress* and *River Music: A Flyfisher's Four Seasons*. The son of a lunatic-fringe fly fisherman and the brother of a professional fly tier, fly-fishing guide, and bamboo-rod builder, Jim grew up fly fishing in the mountains of eastern Tennessee. Since 1972 he has lived in midcoast Maine, where he has worked variously as a lobster fisherman, truck driver, boating and fishing writer, and editor of books about fishing, boats, ships, and the sea.

IF YOU GO

▶ **Prime Time:** The fishing season runs from mid-June to early September. The brookies feed aggressively throughout the short summer at this latitude.

▶ **Getting There:** The camps operated by Three Rivers Lodge on the Woods River are 150 miles from Labrador City, accessible only by floatplane from Wabush or Labrador City, which are served by Air Canada (888-247-2262). Please note that you'll need to pack carefully, as there's a forty-pound luggage restriction for the floatplane ride into Three Rivers.

▶ **Accommodations:** Three Rivers Lodge (781-246-2527; www.trophylabrador.com) is the best and only bet on the Woods River. They operate a main lodge as well as several fly-in outpost camps. The guides at Three Rivers are extremely knowledgeable, and the hosts at the lodge are first rate, offering excellent meals and comfortable cabins. Most fishing is accessed via boats or outboard-powered canoes; two days of fly-in fishing are included in the package. The trip runs just under $4,000, not including airfare to Labrador City.

▶ **Equipment:** The brook trout of the Woods River system are big and strong and require sturdy sticks. While a 6-weight rod might do the job, you'd be better off with 9-foot outfits in 7- or 8-weights, loaded with floating line. Leaders should be 9-foot, tapered from 1x to 3x; bring tippet material in 5- to 10-pound test. While fish are somewhat sensitive to fly size if a hatch is occurring, they are not terribly particular about patterns. Standbys for Labrador brookies include Royal Wulffs (#8–#10), Quill Duns (#14–#16), Green Drakes (#8–#10), dark Woolly Buggers (#4–#6), and weighted Muddler Minnows (#4–#6).

22

DESTINATION

REDFISH AROUND COCODRIE

RECOMMENDED BY **Sonny Mahan**

Little known as a fishing quarry outside of the southern United States, redfish are one of the most popular, if not *the* most popular, sport fish sought by saltwater anglers south of the Mason-Dixon line. Dubbed the poor man's bonefish by some, redfish (a member of the drum family) have many recommendable traits. They are plentiful, they will spend a good deal of time in shallower water close to shore, they are tenacious fighters, and they are very willing to take a fly. Sonny Mahan has devoted a good deal of time to chasing redfish in his native Texas, but his favorite spot to pursue the species that was almost obliterated by one chef's obsession with Cajun spices is an hour south of New Orleans, at a place called Cocodrie.

"Down at Cocodrie, the fishing is back in the marsh country," Sonny explained. "You're about twenty miles in from the coast. It's nothing to go back in there and see seventy-five tails up in the air. You're poling along in a traditional flats boat, just as though you were fishing for bones in the Bahamas. Except you're back in the marsh, and there are alligators, ducks, spoonbill, and lots of reds." Most redfishing along the Gulf coast takes place on flatslike environments, around bays and estuaries. It's a sight-fishing game; many times, anglers can stalk the fish on foot. The softer bottom of the marshes, and the presence of those toothed reptiles, make wading impractical at Cocodrie. All fishing is done from the boat, though anglers still cast predominately to sighted fish.

The redfish (sometimes called red drum, puppy drum, or bull drum) can easily be recognized by the one or more black spots on its upper flank near the base of the tail. Their sobriquet is somewhat misleading, as redfish tend toward an iridescent silvery gray, with a coppery patina on the back and upper sides. Redfish are sought by fly anglers close to shore, though they tend to move to offshore waters as they get bigger. They can reach a maximum length of 5 feet and weigh up to 100 pounds, though the fish encountered by fly anglers tend to be much smaller. Redfish are liberal feeders, favoring bottom-dwelling species such as crabs, shrimp, and sand dollars; larger redfish will feed on menhaden, mullet, and other forage fish. Anglers love to come upon them with their signature black-dotted tail up in the air, as a feeding redfish is a willing redfish. If redfish aren't actively feeding they can be extremely difficult to entice into striking. Redfish that see a lot of angling pressure can be every bit as wary as bonefish.

Around the marshes of Cocodrie, the redfish tend to key on shrimp that go into the brackish water to spawn, as well as on crabs and mullet. "Each pocket of marsh drains through a canal that was developed from the oil-field days," Sonny said. "Each pocket is almost like a pond, and it's just one pond after another. There's lots of grass. It's almost like bass fishing. Some of the fish seem to be resident, some come and go with the tide. We'll try to find fish that are feeding or at least cruising."

When Sonny encounters a large group of feeding redfish at Cocodrie, he tries to fish the edges. "We can get seven or eight fish from the pod that way, without spooking them," he explained. Casting a shrimp or crab pattern in front of a fish, letting it sink, and then slowly retrieving it so it drifts off the bottom near the fish's head will often provoke a strike. Strip strikes – like in bonefishing – are the best way to set the hook. When shrimp or crab patterns are not producing, many redfish anglers will fall back on spoon flies. Spoon flies resemble, well, the spoons fished by spin fishermen. Tied with a weed guard, however, they can be deadly. Cruising fish can also sometimes be enticed to take a popping bug. "If you put it out in front of them," Sonny said, "they'll put out a V-wake. You've got to keep it moving until they hit it. When they decide they want it, they really blow up on it." Once you get them on the line, redfish are gritty, if not flashy fighters. "More bulldog than greyhound," Sonny quipped; other redfish aficionados have described their fighting capabilities as comparable to that of a 30-pound bonefish with the endurance of a tuna. Most marsh fish are in the 3- to 15- pound class.

"When the sun is coming up on the bayou and I'm pulling into one of those ponds with scores of tails sticking up in the air, I feel like I'm one of the chosen few," Sonny mused. "Most of the thrill is seeing the fish, making the cast, and getting him to eat the fly. The rest of it, I don't care."

SONNY MAHAN has been fly fishing since 1995. He learned his fly-casting skills from Lefty Kreh. Sonny fishes extensively for redfish along the Texas and Louisiana coasts and regularly seeks a variety of saltwater species in Florida. He conducts casting clinics around Texas in association with Sage.

IF YOU GO

▶ **Prime Time:** Fall is generally the best time to be at Cocodrie, as the weather has cooled a bit and the fish are on the feed. If you can take the heat, fish can be caught regularly throughout the spring and summer.

▶ **Getting There:** Cocodrie is about an hour's drive south of New Orleans.

▶ **Accommodations:** It's not difficult to make a day trip down to Cocodrie from New Orleans should a convention or other engagement bring you there. For a taste of life in the Terrebonne Parish, you can stay at Sportsman's Paradise (985-594-7772; www.sports mansparadisecocodrie.com) in Chauvin, Louisiana. The lodge has a restaurant in addition to rooms.

▶ **Equipment:** A 9-foot, 8-weight rod equipped with floating line and 100 yards of backing, completed with a 9-foot leader tapered to 12- or 15-pound test, will work well in the marshes of Cocodrie. Standby patterns include spoon flies (like Cave's Wobbler), Clouser Deep Minnows, Lefty's Deceivers, and a variety of crab and shrimp patterns. You should also bring along a few poppers. Blaine Townsend of Sportsman's Paradise is a highly regarded Cocodrie guide, and he leads trips for two anglers for $350. Danny Ayo (985-868-7208; www.flyfishlouisiana.com) also leads fly-fishing trips in the region's plentiful marshes.

LANDLOCKED SALMON ON THE WEST BRANCH OF THE PENOBSCOT RIVER

RECOMMENDED BY **Bucky Owen**

The landlocked salmon is the state fish of Maine. It is native to four river basins in the state, and is now present in fishable numbers in nearly three hundred lakes and more than forty rivers and streams. Landlocks evolved from spawning Atlantic salmon that were trapped inland due to geologic unrest some ten thousand years ago. While smaller than their oceangoing brethren, landlocked salmon bear the same genetic makeup as *Salmo salar* and have the same proclivity for acrobatics once they feel the steel. Bucky Owen has fished for landlocks in many of the lakes and streams of Maine, and he has special feelings for the West Branch of the Penobscot. "I first fished the West Branch in 1968 for three days in the fall, with my boss at the time," Bucky recalled. "I've been going back ever since. My old boss is still going too, and he's in his eighties."

The Penobscot is New England's second-largest river system, with its West Branch rising near Penobscot Lake on the Maine/Quebec border, and the headwaters of the East Branch beginning at East Branch Pond. The mainstem of the river, which empties into Penobscot Bay near the town of Bucksport, once hosted sizable runs of Atlantic salmon. Today the runs are tremendously diminished. In the 1800s, the Penobscot was a prime conduit for transporting logs out of the great north woods, making Bangor the "timber capital of the world."

The West Branch of the Penobscot has two sections of interest to fly anglers seeking landlocked salmon: the upper and lower segments. The lower section pours out of Ripogenus Dam and gets a good deal of angler attention. Many consider the thirty-five miles from the dam to the town of Millinocket, which is paralleled by a road for its length, among the best landlock waters in New England. Despite the road, it's a splendid section of river, punctuated with some hairy white water and offering spectacular vistas

of Mount Katahdin in Baxter State Park, which borders the southern sections of this stretch. Because of the cooler water temperatures that the dam releases maintain, the Lower West Branch can fish fairly well throughout the summer, though the landlocks are most active during spring and fall. The Upper West Branch of the Penobscot flows into Chesuncook Lake (which is impounded by Ripogenus) from Seboomook Lake. This river corridor is wilderness country, immortalized by Thoreau in *The Maine Woods*; it's still one of the best places in Maine to encounter moose up close and personal. "We've had monstrous bulls block us in the river, right in the middle of the rut," Bucky recalled. The Upper West Branch is a September fishery, as anglers key on landlocks moving up from the lake to spawn.

Smelt are a primary food source for landlocked salmon, and swinging smelt imitations remains a popular tactic on landlock rivers like the West Branch. A number of famous streamer patterns were first tied in Maine to mimic this baitfish. Best known among these patterns is the Gray Ghost, which was created by Carrie Stevens in 1924. Gray Ghosts and other streamers are fished down and across on the West Branch, with a strip as the fly begins to swing. Runs with lots of boulders tend to hold the most fish; larger fish often will be found just below fast water. "The fish are very aggressive, especially in the fall," Bucky said. "They'll take a fly really hard, and then they'll put on a great show. You'll often get six, seven, eight jumps out of a fish before you get him in." Where streamers produce best early and late in the season, the late spring and summer can see some intense insect activity, with mayfly hatches beginning in early June, caddis following later in the month and stretching through August, and stoneflies appearing in July. Both nymphs and surface patterns will take fish. Landlocks will run as large as 8 pounds in the West Branch, though a 5-pound salmon is considered a good catch. Most fish run in the 14- to 17-inch class. With the right conditions and a good guide, an experienced angler has a good chance to have ten hookups in a day's fishing.

Pristine north woods beauty and enough good water to provide a degree of solitude for those willing to seek it make the West Branch of the Penobscot worth a visit anytime during the fishing season. For Bucky, however, it's early fall days on the upper river that define the West Branch landlocked salmon experience. "We camp up there, and it generally gets below freezing at night. When you wake up, there's mist on the river and the smell of campfires. We float in traditional canoes made of wood and canvas. Mine were built by a fellow named Doc Blanchard, a wildlife biologist from the region who was

OPPOSITE:
Dawn can be
a magic time
to cast a fly on
the West
Branch of the
Penobscot.

24

DESTINATION

111

renowned for his boat building. You're on the river and there's ice in your guides. The sun burns the mist off, and you see the brilliant fall foliage. You paddle your canoe into one of the pools, make a cast, the fly swings behind a rock, and a fish slams it and goes airborne. That's what it's all about."

BUCKY OWEN served as commissioner of Maine's Department of Fisheries and Wildlife for four years, before retiring in 1997. He was a professor of wildlife ecology at the University of Maine (Orono) for thirty-three years and served as the department chair for ten years. Bucky is very active in conservation projects and currently serves as chair of the Maine chapter of the Nature Conservancy. He has fished throughout Maine, and has also traveled to fish the Maritime Provinces of Canada, the western United States, Alaska, and the Northwest Territories.

IF YOU GO

▶ **Prime Time:** The West Branch of the Penobscot is open from April 1 to September 30. Late May through early July is the most consistent time to fish the Lower West Branch. September is the time to be on the Upper West Branch.

▶ **Getting There:** Millinocket, which is at the bottom of the Lower West Branch, is five and a half hours north of Boston. Count on another hour or so to get to Ripogenus Dam, and another hour to reach the Upper West Branch.

▶ **Accommodations:** If you're fishing the Upper West Branch, you'll need to camp. If you're fishing the Lower West Branch, several lodging options are available. See a comprehensive listing at www.maineguide.com/millinocket.

▶ **Equipment:** A 9-foot 6-weight rod is ideal for landlocked salmon; it should be outfitted with both floating and sinking lines, with 100 yards of backing. Nine-foot leaders tapered to 4x should be adequate, with tippet material in 3- to 6-pound test. Popular streamers include Gray Ghosts, Black Ghosts, and Mickey Finns, in #6 to #12. Dan Legere at Maine Guide Fly Shop (207-695-2266; www.maineguideflyshop.com) knows the upper river well; his shop offers multiday floats for $225/per day per person (three-day minimum). Ian Cameron of Penobscot Driftboats (207-942-3234) leads drift-boat floats on the lower river, including the Ripogenus Gorge.

STRIPED BASS OFF

MARTHA'S VINEYARD

RECOMMENDED BY **Bucky Burrows**

The carved wooden fish that hangs in the old State House near Faneuil Hall in Boston is a cod. If Bay State sport fishers had it their way, it would be a striper. Striped bass are hands down the favorite target of New England saltwater fly fishers. Before politicos and celebrities descended upon Martha's Vineyard to see and be seen, anglers recognized the island as one of the best places anywhere to pursue stripers big and small.

Located seven miles off the coast of Cape Cod, the Vineyard boasts nearly 125 miles of tidal shoreline, shoreline riddled with boulders that provide ideal striper habitat. Anglers can approach fish by land from beaches, estuaries, reefs, points, and inlets on the north side of the island. Access to a boat, of course, opens up offshore rips and other islands to the angler's flies.

Bucky Burrows likes to hunt stripers from the casting deck of his eighteen-foot Boston Whaler. "When fly fishing surfaced back around '89, I was ready. I'd fished for stripers on the Vineyard with conventional gear for a while, and fly fishing posed more of a challenge."

Fly fishing for stripers has been around for some time – there's evidence that suggests that statesman Daniel Webster caught striped bass on the Potomac with streamers circa 1810. However, the skill and stamina necessary to toss big flies into the wind and sink them down quickly was beyond most anglers. Stout (but light) fast-action graphite rods and more sophisticated shooting-head fly lines developed in the last decade have made fly fishing for stripers a bit easier ... and folks along the Eastern Seaboard, frustrated with the crowds on scant trout streams and piqued by the challenges of fishing the salt, have taken to it like gangbusters.

Much of Bucky's fishing takes place on the north shore of the Vineyard and around

the Elizabeth Islands. Most fishing is sight-fishing – though it's generally not stripers that the anglers will see. "There are a lot of spots where baitfish congregate, and where stripers are sure to appear," Bucky explained. "Rips – places where the current works against a reef or rocks to create a pocket of calm water where stripers can lie in ambush – and big sandbars. If there's a bunch of birds on the water, you can guess that something attracted their interest. Perhaps baitfish that were scared up to the surface by feeding stripers. Sometimes we'll see squid jumping three feet clear of the water, and there will be bass waiting below them. There's no guesswork involved there."

When such a feeding melee is encountered, the angler casts a big fly into the middle of the frenzy – a sand eel or squid pattern, perhaps – and strips like crazy. If the water is calm, a surface fly like a gurgler will work. The takes are not subtle. In these situations, the bass are not examining the fly too closely. Most fly-caught fish are in the 8- to 10-pound class, though each year trophies in the 40- to 50-pound range are encountered.

Casting to stripers is not light work. Throwing a 9- or 10-weight rod and a 450-grain shooting head a consistent forty-five or fifty feet can quickly wear the uninitiated out. "A lot of newcomers are shot after four hours," Bucky admitted. "Being consistent with your casting is extremely important. The guy who can keep his fly in the zone for the longest time is going to catch the most fish."

One of the biggest challenges facing striper anglers off the Vineyard is the wind. One has to adapt to the wind as it shifts about in order to keep the fly in the bait zone – and keep it out of one's scalp. Controlling stripped fly line in the boat can also be testing. "Between the rocking boat, coils of line at your feet, and mentally gearing up to make the cast, there's a lot going on, and many people get overwhelmed," Bucky said. "Throw in the excitement of a school of boiling stripers, and people get pretty flustered."

A stealthy approach is also important. "A lot of clients don't realize that they're shifting their weight as they cast – fish pick this up," Bucky added. "When the fish realizes that there's something in the water bigger than they are, like a boat, they shift out of the predator mode, into the defensive. They're suddenly scared, and they don't eat."

For a change of pace, Bucky will also fish little coves, tight against the shore, with lighter tackle. "Decent-sized fish – twenty-four to thirty inches – will often hold in just two to three feet of water. They are a lot of fish on a seven- or eight-weight rod."

The Vineyard's proximity to the Gulf Stream brings a number of other fly-rod species within reach. Toothy bluefish pass by in the springtime and return in the middle of

OPPOSITE:
Fly fishers
on Martha's
Vineyard can
chase stripers
by land
or by sea.

August. Atlantic bonito show up from mid-July to October, and false albacore are present in September. When the false albacore arrive, they're an especially desirable target. "The schools are small, and extremely fast moving," Bucky described. "When they hit bait they rip it up, and then continue. Trying to present a fly to them is like trying to hit a Roger Clemens fastball. Sometimes they move in patterns. If you can discern the pattern, you can lie in wait, and time your next cast in the sequence. Anticipating their arrival is incredibly exciting."

BUCKY BURROWS worked as a commercial fisherman and bush pilot in Alaska from 1973 to 1990. In the mid-seventies, he bought property on Martha's Vineyard and fished there as often as possible on break from Alaska. Bucky began guiding on the Vineyard in 1992, and he especially enjoys introducing trout anglers to the excitement of saltwater fly fishing. When he's not guiding on the Vineyard, Bucky can be found skiing and trout fishing the West from a home base in Alta, Utah.

DESTINATION 25

IF YOU GO

▶ **Prime Time:** Striper fishing is most consistent from May to July 4, and then again from early September to as late as Thanksgiving.

▶ **Getting There:** Most travelers reach Martha's Vineyard via ferry, like the Steamship Authority (www.steamshipauthority.com). Cape Air (800-352-0714; www.flycapeair.com) offers regularly scheduled flights.

▶ **Accommodations:** The Vineyard offers many quaint inn options. Among them are the Hob Knob Inn (800-696-2723; www.hobknob.com) and Edgartown Inn (508-627-4794; www.edgartowninn.com).

▶ **Equipment:** Most anglers prefer 9-foot 9-, 10-, or 11-weight rods. Bring a floating line, an intermediate sinking line, and an extra-fast sinking line. Nine-foot leaders with a 10- to 20-pound tippet work for most situations; for bigger fish, a shock tippet of 30- to 50-pound test is advisable. Squid patterns, Clousers, Lefty's Deceivers, and sand eel patterns in size 1/0 and larger should do the trick; bring a few poppers and gurglers too. Guides who work the Vineyard include Bucky Burrows (508-693-8431); Jaime Boyle (508-693-7454); and Jeff Sayre (508-693-4841; www.flyfishingthevineyard. com). Guides generally have appropriate rods if you do not.

LARGEMOUTH BASS ON
LAKE HUITES

RECOMMENDED BY **Duane Dahlgren**

Largemouth bass (*Micropterus salmoides*) are America's game fish. Upward of 30 million anglers pursue the bass each year, casting some $50 billion into what's become very big business. Some trout fishermen are inclined to look askance at bass angling; those boats, those ultracompetitive tournaments, and those hokey Saturday morning programs can be *a bit* tacky. Put those same troutists on a tranquil, scenic lake, have them cast a popping bug into some reeds, and watch a 5-pound bucketmouth inhale it and odds are good they'll feel quite differently. That's what Lake Huites does for fly fishers who may never have had the inkling to pursue bass. It adds a touch of class to what is ultimately a simple, visceral, but very pleasurable pursuit. After all, can 30 million Americans be wrong?

"A lot of places you fly fish are pretty beautiful," Duane Dahlgren said, reflecting on a recent trip to Huites. "This spot is drop-dead gorgeous in a stark, minimalist way. Add to that constant action with good-sized fish – and the potential for every cast to bring a double-digit fish on – and you have the makings of a great trip."

Lake Huites is located on the western edge of Mexico in the foothills of the Sierra Madre, just south of the spectacular Copper Canyon area. "Real *Treasure of the Sierra Madre* country, complete with old gold mines," Duane said. It is a man-made impoundment, formed when the Rio Fuerte was dammed in 1994. The lake is quite long, measuring thirty thousand acres and thirty miles. It was stocked with Florida-strain largemouth fingerlings, and the fish have thrived and multiplied in Huites's clear waters, fattening up on tilapia, shad, and just about any other protein they can catch. Where some Mexican bass lakes have suffered from rampant commercial fishing, Lake Huites should be spared such a fate; it's the first lake in Mexico with laws protecting bass from commercial fishing. Fish average 2.5 to 3 pounds, with many fish in the 5- to 8-pound range and real lunkers over 10 pounds caught regularly. As anyone who's flipped past one of those Saturday morning shows knows, largemouth bass like structure. Lake Huites gives them plenty. Steep canyon walls slope into the water at many places and, where the shoreline is not canyon-lined, there's thick brush and trees. Numerous rocky points provide additional shelter.

Largemouths are not regaled for their fighting endurance, but their "I'll eat anything I can get my mouth around" aggressiveness makes for dramatic takes, often punctuated by belly-flopping jumps. When conditions present themselves so fish are willing to take a popper or deer hair bug on the surface, it simply doesn't get much better. "There were times when we'd be cruising along a brushy shoreline, casting white poppers up against the bank," Duane recalled, "and it seemed like I was getting a fish on every other cast. They wore my white poppers out. No matter how many you get, every take is a thrill. The fish weren't huge; they probably averaged a little over two pounds. That's enough bass to be fun on a fly rod, especially when they're feeding on top. I was there in February, and the fish weren't quite on their spawning beds yet. The time to be there with a fly rod is the spring, when they're in the shallows and feeling especially territorial and mean."

When poppers aren't producing, tying on a streamer pattern and fishing drop-offs will keep you in fish. Anglers intent on taking a real trophy will want to consider switching to a sinking line and fishing deep structure. The guides at Lake Huites, while not very conversant in English, speak bass very well and can put you where the big fish have been caught on spinning gear. During the "off-season," Duane was able to coax twenty-five to thirty fish out of the lake a day. "And that was with a siesta after lunch and a fair amount of time trying to get my dad into a ten-pounder on spinning gear," Duane added. "Some of the guys with conventional tackle will pull a hundred fish out in a day. Under the right conditions, I don't see why that wouldn't be possible with a fly rig."

In June 2001, celebrated angling personality Flip Pallot brought a film crew to Lake Huites to see if fly fishing for bass could make good material for his ESPN program *Walker's Cay Chronicles*. By all accounts, the filming was a success. "This might be the finest bass-fishing show ever shot using fly rods instead of plug rods," Flip said. "The fish are aggressive and will readily attack an assortment of surface flies." Perhaps there is hope for those Saturday morning bass shows.

DUANE DAHLGREN received his first fly rod at the age of ten and has chased bass, trout, steelhead, and many saltwater species in the forty years since. His angling adventures have taken him to New Zealand, British Columbia, the Bahamas, the Caymans, and Belize, as well as across the American West. A geologist by trade, Duane is also a partner in Yellowdog Flyfishing Adventures (www.yellowdogflyfishing.com).

IF YOU GO

▶ **Prime Time:** In late March, April, and May, the fish are on their spawning beds in the shallows and are especially susceptible to surface presentations. The season is open September through June. One caution: lake levels fluctuate at times, and a serious drawdown or rise in water can put the fish off the bite for a bit.

▶ **Getting There:** Lake Huites Lodge is in Sinaloa, Mexico, and is accessed from Los Mochis. Most anglers fly to Los Mochis from Tucson, Arizona, on AeroCalifornia (800-AERO-CAL). Guests are transported the three and a half hours from Los Mochis to the lodge in air-conditioned vans. This area is not overly Americanized, and gives visitors a sense of the "real" Mexico. Hold on tight for the last hour, when winding up an unpaved road that tends to keep less adventurous anglers away.

▶ **Accommodations:** The recently constructed Lake Huites Lodge (888-744-8867; www.lakehuiteslodge.com) caters to spin and fly anglers. The rooms are comfortable if not opulent, and the hearty Mexican food is good and plentiful. Beer and margaritas flow indefinitely as part of the package. A four-night/three-day fishing stay is $1,195, and this includes everything except airfare to Mochis. Capacity is twenty anglers.

▶ **Equipment:** A 9-foot 7- or 8-weight rod is the best choice. If conditions are right, you'll need only floating line, though it's best to bring a sinking line as well if the lake levels go up; some like bass-taper lines to turn over big poppers. Nine-foot bass leaders tapered to 0x with tippet in the 12- to 20-pound class will stand up to heavy fish. Your box should include surface flies like Umpqua Swimmin' Frog, Dahlberg Divers, Loudmouth Poppers, Crystal Poppers, and Snook-A-Roo. Also include subsurface flies: Burk's Flat Tailed Worm, Swimmin' Waterdog, Zonkers, Hot Claw Crayfish, Burk's Bass Flash, Randy's Gator Frog, Whit's Sheep Flies, and Lefty's Deceivers. All patterns should have weedguards so they can be fished around cover.

SNOOK OFF BOCA PAILA

RECOMMENDED BY **Cathy Beck**

Snook (*Centropomus undecimalis*) are an increasingly popular fly-rod species, noteworthy for their great strength and a curiosity that borders on the playful. They are marked by a distinct black line that runs laterally along both flanks and by an exaggerated underbite that belies a propensity for malice, at least if you're a baitfish or a fly. Snook are indigenous to the east and west coasts of Florida and throughout Central America, and they generally prefer brackish waters along shoreline structure (they can survive in both all-fresh and all-salt water). The creek-fed mangrove swamps surrounding Boca Paila on Mexico's Yucatán Peninsula provide ideal snook habitat and regularly produce fish topping 20 pounds.

Cathy Beck caught her first snook on the Yucatán a dozen years ago, while pursuing tarpon. She's been back every year since. "I was new to fly fishing in salt water. A lodge owner named Dial Duncan invited Barry and me down to fish for tarpon in some ocean-fed lakes near the bottom of the Yucatán Peninsula. It turned out that there were huge snook in the lake as well, near 'blue holes' where the salt water entered. I caught three snook there in three days, twenty-two, twenty-three, and twenty-five pounds – the biggest snook I've ever caught in my life." At Boca, most of the snook fishing is done from a boat around the mangrove islands. The fish are generally up tight against the mangroves, in shallow water. Anglers will cruise the edge of an island and look for the shapes of fish in among the roots. Other times, the water might not be clear enough to spot them, and you'll blind-cast to places where snook have been encountered before. A big popper smacked up against the mangroves will sometimes bring them charging out. "You can forget the precise, technical stuff in the mangroves," Cathy said. "Just slap it in there. More than once when we come up to a likely spot and don't see any fish, our guide will

OPPOSITE:
Steering
a big snook
out of the
mangroves
around Boca
Paila can
take some
muscle.

121

splash the water with his pole, and the snook will come out to have a look."

The snook's unpredictability is one of its greatest appeals. At times you can literally smack the fish on the head with the fly and it'll refuse to respond. There are other times when a fish seems to be almost anticipating the angler's arrival, and is eager to check out the fly as soon as you stop the boat and cast. "It's a thrill to find a big snook that wants to play," Cathy said. "He'll follow the blue and white Deceiver, and then suddenly turn around and refuse it. It's almost like he's arrogant. Tie on a black Deceiver, and he might grab it … and maybe you'll grab it out of his mouth. That doesn't mean that the game is over. If you show him something else, he might come out again and grab it. Since the water is shallow and relatively clear, you get to watch everything happen. Getting the fish to play with you is as much fun as hooking one."

Which isn't to say that the battle with a snook is anticlimactic. Snook are notoriously strong fighters. They're not big runners but they thrash and jump – or make a beeline for the mangroves. Even with a 10-weight rod and a 60-pound shock tippet, it can be tough to control them if they decide to seek cover. While snook are a primary attraction for Cathy, Boca Paila is even more celebrated for its permit (up to 20 pounds) and bonefish (average 2 to 3 pounds). Juvenile tarpon are present year-round, and larger migratory fish often arrive in the summer and fall. (Dozens of Grand Slams – landing a tarpon, bonefish, and permit in one day – are scored at Boca each year.) The lodge is within twenty yards of the beach and two hundred yards of a large lagoon and miles of flats that eventually bottom out into Ascension Bay. "The lagoon is protected from the wind," Cathy explained. "There has to be a hurricane before you can't go fishing there. As a result, you're never left in the lodge reading a book."

Boca Paila is situated in the midst of the 1.3-million-acre Sian Ka'an Biosphere Reserve, providing a respite from the "Cancúnization" some parts of the Yucatán are experiencing. Miles of pristine white sand beaches, snorkeling possibilities along the Palancar Reef, and the chance to visit the Mayan ruins of Tulum (forty minutes north of the lodge) provide enough diversions to please nonangling accomplices.

Once the packing is done for your Yucatán adventure, Cathy advises that you remove one thing from your bags – preconceptions. "I think it's extremely important for anglers to leave preset ideas at home. If you go thinking, 'I'm not going home without a tarpon or a permit,' you might be disappointed, as weather and water conditions might not be conducive to tarpon or permit fishing. It's best to travel with an open mind. If your guide says, 'Let's go for bonefish,' go for bonefish. If the guide says, 'Fish for tarpon,' fish for tarpon. The Boca Paila region has such an incredible variety of sportfishing species, there's always something there. I always try to enjoy what's available."

CATHY BECK and her husband, Barry, conduct fly-fishing schools, clinics, and presentations and lead fly-fishing trips to fresh- and saltwater destinations around the world. Their photographs appear regularly in sporting calendars and magazines, including *Fly Fisherman* and *Field & Stream* (see www.barryandcathybeck.com). The Becks' books include *Cathy Beck's Fly Fishing Handbook, Seasons of the Bighorn* (written with George Kelly), *Fly Fishing the Flats,* and *Favorite Pennsylvania Fly Water.*

IF YOU GO

▶ **Prime Time:** Snook are present throughout the year, though numbers fluctuate due to water conditions ... hence the importance of being ready to chase other species as well.

▶ **Getting There:** Boca Paila is situated on the southeast coast of Mexico's Yucatán Peninsula, about 130 miles south of Cancún and 20 miles north of Ascension Bay. Travelers can choose from direct, relatively short flights from many major U.S. cities to Cancún. A pleasant two-and-a-half-hour drive down the coastline concludes your journey to the peaceful seclusion of Boca Paila.

▶ **Accommodations:** Boca Paila Lodge features oceanfront bungalows (with private baths) situated on a spectacular white sand beach. Cuisine is a mix of Mexican, American, and Mayan dishes, with an emphasis on seafood. Seven-night/six-day fishing packages (including transfer from Cancún/room/lodging/guides) are $2,800 per person, based on double occupancy; summer season rates are $1,960. There's a sixteen-person capacity per week.

▶ **Equipment:** A 9-foot 9- or 10-weight rod with floating line and sinking line (the latter for fishing the mouths of creeks) will work for both snook and permit. Your reels should have plenty of backing – 200 yards or more. A short 20-pound tippet with 12 inches of 60-pound shock tippet will help you keep your snook out of the mangroves. For flies, bring Gaines Poppers (in yellow/red and blue/white), Lefty's Deceivers (red/yellow and green/white), Seaducers (yellow/red), Comb's Sea Habits (green/white), and Clouser Minnows (shiner and chartreuse/white), all in size #2/0.

BROWN TROUT ON THE
AU SABLE RIVER

RECOMMENDED BY **Robert M. Linsenman**

There are times when the living waters of a river commingle with the sustaining blood pumping through an angler's heart, to the point where the two are no longer distinguishable. Bob Linsenman knows that feeling.

"I've been fortunate enough to fish many of the world's greatest waters. But wherever I was, I was always wondering what was going on back on the Au Sable, where my family had a cabin when I was a boy. I couldn't stand being away from this river, so a dozen years ago I quit my job in Minneapolis and came back."

The Au Sable bubbles up near Frederic, Michigan, gains water from the north and south branches of the Au Sable and numerous feeder creeks, then winds some two hundred miles southeast, where it dumps into Lake Huron. The river holds brook, rainbow, and brown trout in good numbers in its upper reaches and then increasingly gives way to browns, which decrease in density but increase in size as you proceed downstream. In the early spring, the last ten miles of the river host one of the Great Lakes' great – and most underrated – steelhead runs. The Au Sable's spring creek qualities create a rich potpourri of insect life, making for a diverse and ever-changing trout smorgasbord. Hatches of Hendricksons, Brown Drakes, and *Hexagenia limbata* are especially noteworthy.

The Au Sable's hub town, Grayling, seems oddly named today. In the 1890s, it was grayling that brought anglers to northern Michigan from around the globe; grayling, and also the lumber boom. Both had a profound impact on the river. "Sportsmen" slaughtered grayling by the hundreds each day, for all intents and purposes obliterating the species from the river. Logs harvested from the area were transported down the river, scouring out the river bottom to help create the sandy environs anglers encounter today.

At the time that the timber barons and their cohorts were doing their best to decimate the Au Sable, brook, rainbow, and brown trout were introduced, bearing hope for the future. Since they are a little more wary than grayling, the trout survived the onslaught from points south to create the river's second great fishing epoch. The Michiganders who now steward the river are not about to repeat earlier mistakes. Many interested parties have gathered together to successfully institute a "fly only/no-kill area" on the "Holy Water" stretch. In fact, it was concerned Au Sable anglers who formed the first Trout Unlimited Chapter in 1959, at the bank-side home of famed angler George Griffith.

As befitting a river of its lineage, the Au Sable offers anglers a great variety of experiences. When most visitors think of the Au Sable, they think of the Holy Water – the stretch of river from Burton's Landing (below the confluence of the east and west branches) to Wakely Bridge. The notoriety is well deserved. Tree-lined banks and clear water make it an incredibly beautiful stretch. The river is fairly small at this point, the wading is easy, and this stretch is filled with brookies and some large browns and rainbows. "My ideal experience on the Holy Water would be a morning or evening in May," Bob said, "and I would fish dries – probably Hendricksons or Brown Drakes – to freely rising fish. If there weren't too many canoes on the water, a competent angler would have a good chance to land ten to twenty fish. Out of a dozen fish, four or five would be in the fourteen- to eighteen-inch class."

Another great but very different experience is fishing the Au Sable's hexagenia hatch, which comes off in late June and early July and is largely a nocturnal game. At this latitude, it's still light enough to tie a fly on at ten-thirty. Fishing can continue until one or two in the morning. There's good hex water throughout the river – the lower Holy Water, the north and south branches, and the Big Water down to Mio. For the hex hatch, most people fish from boats – either an Au Sable riverboat or a McKenzie-style drift boat will do.

There are some special challenges facing anglers during the hex hatch, such as learning to cast to fish that you can hear but can't see and overcoming "buck fever." "The best way to get a grasp on judging casting distance and executing casts is to practice," Bob advised. "Put a bag over your head, have a friend stand twenty or thirty feet away and clap, and try to cast the fly six feet to the 'upstream' side of them. You have to be pretty precise. Fish that are positioned in a certain feeding lane won't detour for a fly that floats outside the lane."

Buck fever can be a little tougher to combat. "When the big browns are feeding on those big mayflies, it sounds like a Labrador retriever was dropped in the water. Some of these fish are eight or nine pounds. Visitors are often casting to the biggest fish they've ever had a chance to take on a dry fly, and their blood is boiling. They fall apart. Helping them direct their casts isn't nearly as important as trying to keep them calm. After all, any cast in the Au Sable can mean the catch of a lifetime."

To improve your odds on the Au Sable, you might consider a pre-fishing pilgrimage to the Fisherman's Chapel, located on the Mason Tract section of the Au Sable's south branch. The chapel was funded by George Mason, who dearly loved the river and also donated eleven productive river miles for public access.

In the heat of the hex hatch, anglers will often congregate après-fishing at one of the popular taverns along the river corridor: Spike's Keg O' Nails in Grayling, Ma Deeter's in Luzerne, or Northwood Tavern in Mio. "The most common topic of discussion," Bob quipped, "is 'What went wrong?'"

Robert M. Linsenman is an Au Sable fly-fishing guide, literary agent, and highly regarded author. He has fished widely throughout the United States, Canada, Mexico, and the Bahamas. His feature articles have appeared in *Fly Fisherman, American Angler, Wild Steelhead & Salmon, Fly Fishing and Tying Journal, Fly Fisher,* and *Midwest Fly Fishing.* His books include *Michigan Trout Streams: A Fly Angler's Guide* (now in its second edition) and *Great Lakes Steelhead: A Guided Tour for Fly Anglers* (both with Steve Nevala), as well as *The Au Sable River, Modern Streamers for Trophy Trout* (with Kelly Galloup) and the recently published *Michigan Blue Ribbon Fly Fishing Guide.*

IF YOU GO

► **Prime Time:** The Au Sable fishes well in spring, early summer, and fall; in fall, the foliage is outstanding. Many visitors key in on the hexagenia hatch, which occurs in late June/early July. The brown drake hatch in late May/early June also attracts downstaters.

► **Getting There:** Grayling, the region's hub town, is approximately two hundred miles north of Detroit.

► **Accommodations:** Grayling, Roscommon, Luzerne, and Mio all have reasonable accommodations and eateries. Gates Au Sable Lodge (517-348-8462), right on the banks of the river, is a popular destination.

DESTINATION 28

▶ **Equipment:** A 9-foot rod for a 3-, 4-, or 5-weight line will generally suffice. Floating line is used for most circumstances. Fast-sinking tips or sinking lines are helpful in early and late season for fishing streamers to big browns. Nine-foot leaders in 4x or 5x and tippet ranging from 2x to 7x should accommodate most situations. As alluded to above, the Au Sable has prolific and varied insect hatches. While the Hendrickson, Brown Drake, and hexagenia hatches are well chronicled, many other hatches occur. Visit one of the local fly shops to see what's happening before you take off on the water. Many guides serve the area. Bob Linsenman (989-685-3161) leads trips, as do the folks at Gates Au Sable Lodge and the Fly Factory (517-348-5844).

TAIMEN IN MONGOLIA

RECOMMENDED BY **Jeff Vermillion**

There's a story that has circulated among fly fishers that smacks of urban legend. It goes something like this: A few folks are fly fishing a run in Mongolia, and some local herds-men come upon them. They are, not surprisingly, curious. Some sign language is exchanged and the herdsmen understand that the anglers are fishing for taimen. The herdsmen smile and one dismounts from his horse with rifle in hand. The anglers, per-haps recalling tales of Genghis Khan from a far-distant history class, fear the worst. Their fears are misplaced. The gun-toting herdsman soon shoots a groundhog. One of his com-rades joins him with what looks like a grappling hook, impales the groundhog, swings the hook and rodent package over his head on a long rope, and flings it into the middle of the river. Before the carcass has drifted five feet, the water erupts. The herdsmen don't hook up, but the message is clear: *For big fish, use big bait.*

The pursuit of taimen – the world's largest salmonid, capable of reaching 70-plus inches in length and more than 100 pounds – might be characterized as "the next big thing" in the adventure fly-fishing world. Angling is conducted in north-central Mongolia, a region quite similar to Montana's Yellowstone River valley, with the excep-tion that it had not seen a fly rod until Jeff Vermillion and his brothers showed up in 1995. Jeff first became interested in taimen when he was guiding on the Ponoi on the Kola Peninsula. He'd heard tales about fish approaching 100 pounds that were caught on mouse patterns, in Russia, from a guide friend named Max Mamaev. As he tried to plan a trip, he learned that the Russian taimen fisheries were in steep decline. The idea got put on the back burner.

A little later, he learned about Mongolia through a slide presentation. The culture and geography of the area were fascinating, and he'd heard there were taimen there, too, but

*OPPOSITE:
Taimen are the
world's largest
salmonid,
capable of
reaching
70 inches.*

129

figured that the fishery was on its way out as it was in Russia. Eventually he got his hands on a promotional video. One scene showed two fellows gutting a fish they'd killed. It had a dozen mice in its stomach, and Jeff decided he had to go.

"When we finally got there," Jeff said, "one guy caught a taimen on his first cast, about fifteen pounds. We caught a lot of fish like that using streamers. Fun, but not exactly what we'd come for, from a fishing standpoint. At one point I was fishing a cut bank. I put away the streamers and tied on a huge mouse pattern that my friend Max had tied back on the Ponoi when we first started discussing taimen. I was skating the fly across the surface when a huge wake came up from nowhere, and a big taimen – the biggest we'd seen – was trying to hammer the mouse. Finally, it grabbed the fly in an explosion of water. I was too quick on the draw and pulled the fly away. 'Boy, I screwed that up,' I thought. One or two casts later, the fish flew three or four feet out of the water with the mouse pattern – the biggest fish I'd ever had on a fly rod. Eventually, I brought it to hand – fifty-two inches long and a huge girth. Now we had a sense of where the big fish liked to lay. Before the week was out, the other guys all got into fish over fifty inches."

Once indigenous to much of northern Eurasia, the taimen's range is now limited to remote sections of Russia and Mongolia. What they may lack in comeliness, taimen compensate for in ferocity. Visitors can leave their nymphs and emergers at home; these fish want real protein, in the form of rodents, fish, and even ducks. "I'd say ninety percent of the fishing we do is with mouse patterns," Jeff continued. "Some of it is sight-fishing. Many times the fish will follow the fly across the current, slashing at it. This is disconcerting, as the head of a bigger fish is the size of a human head. The take of a big taimen is not something you'll forget soon after."

Once hooked, taimen will sometimes jump clear of the water several times before dogging down. Jeff equates their fight with that of a brown trout – albeit a very big brown trout. Hooking into a taimen in the 40- to 50-inch class is not a sure thing in Mongolia, though such fish are caught each week during the season. "I would compare odds to those on a good steelhead river," Jeff added. "You might not get any opportunities one day, you might get ten the next. Over the course of a week, you'll have a number of cracks at a big fish."

A taimen adventure offers the chance to experience firsthand the epoch-old nomadic culture of the Mongolian herdsmen, who dwell in *gers* (yurts) that they erect and break down as they move across the land. "The people are very generous, and very fun to be

DESTINATION

29

around," Jeff said. "If you approach a *ger*, odds are you'll soon be invited in for a meal." If you're very lucky, you may have the opportunity to enjoy a toast with the local cordial of choice: vodka fermented from mare's milk.

For those who tire of taimen, lenok, a salmonid of modest proportions, indigenous to Mongolia and Russia, and grayling, both provide good sport and will rise to traditional trout patterns. If you hook up with a lenok or grayling and let the fish run to a deeper hole, beware; a bit of sport for you makes a great meal for a taimen.

JEFF VERMILLION spent his childhood in Billings, Montana, and Chile and Brazil. Over the years, he worked hard to avoid a "real job" so that he could fish more. Eventually, he and his brothers realized that perhaps a middle ground would be to set up a fly-fishing business, Sweetwater Travel. Jeff has guided in Alaska, Montana, Chile, Brazil, Russia, and Mongolia. He currently lives in Livingston, Montana.

IF YOU GO

▶ **Prime Time:** May 15 to June 20 and August 20 to October 10.

▶ **Getting There:** You'll need to fly into Ulan Bator, Mongolia, which is served from Seoul, Beijing, Osaka, and Moscow. A helicopter will deliver you from Ulan Bator to the river.

▶ **Accommodations:** Sweetwater Travel (800-FISH-BUM; www.sweetwatertravel.com) serves Mongolia. Their program includes riverside accommodations (in *gers* or tents) with hot water, electricity, and other amenities you probably wouldn't expect in outer Mongolia. Guides (and many camp staff) speak English. Mongolian and American-style cuisine is served; mare's milk vodka before or after dinner is optional. Packages excluding airfare to Ulan Bator begin at $5,200. Fish Mongolia (866-427-9668; www.fish mongolia.com) also offers taimen fishing packages.

▶ **Equipment:** A 9-foot rod for 8- or 9-weight line will land most taimen. Floating lines are generally used, though on occasion a sinking line will help reach fish in deeper pools. Your outfitter will provide mouse patterns and streamers appropriate for taimen. For lenok bring a 5-weight rod outfitted with a floating line. Caddis, mayfly, and terrestrial patterns work well for lenok.

DESTINATION

29

BROWN AND RAINBOW TROUT
ON THE BIGHORN RIVER

RECOMMENDED BY **Barry Beck**

Barry Beck still remembers the time he fell in love. "Back in the seventies, my wife Cathy and I used to do a Montana fishing loop each year in our VW van. We'd start in Paradise Valley, go around Yellowstone, then head over to Henry's Fork, then up the Gallatin, spend the last night in Bozeman, and then head home to Pennsylvania. Early on during one of these trips, we happened to spend a night in Hardin. We overheard these guys in a burger joint talking about the fish they were catching on a river called the Bighorn. We decided to check it out.

"We met up with Mike Craig down there and got out on the 'Horn. Next thing we knew, we were calling ahead and canceling all of our other reservations. For the next few weeks, we slept anywhere we could find room to sleep so we could fish the river. One of our first days on the 'Horn, we came upon the greatest Trico hatch we'd ever seen. The hatch was so prolific, you could smell the dead flies in the air. The fish were moving upriver through the insects, like a formation of geese. It sounded like they were eating salad." Needless to say, Barry and Cathy have been visiting the Bighorn ever since.

The Bighorn River as we know it today was created in 1967 with the completion of Yellowtail Dam. The cool, clean water released from the dam nurtures fecund weed growth, which in turn fosters abundant insect life and a climate where fish can propagate and grow quickly. Bighorn rainbows average 16 inches and brown trout average 15 inches, with many larger specimens regularly encountered. In the first few miles of the Bighorn below the dam, populations can approach up to ten thousand fish per mile in good-water years.

Those who equate Montana trout fishing with snowcapped mountains will be a bit taken aback at the Bighorn's environs. Along the western edge of the Great Plains, the surroundings are largely devoid of trees, except for cottonwoods along the banks of the river. Look closer, and you'll appreciate the subtle shadings of the rock escarpments and the not-so-subtle hatches that have made the Bighorn a destination fishery.

Visitors can expect constant hatches throughout the year. Blue-Winged Olives come off in the spring and can be imitated effectively in nymphal stages with Pheasant Tails and in adult stages with Parachute Adams. Come July, little yellow stoneflies appear and provide slightly easier fishing, as fish seek the insects in the faster water. With August, Pale Morning Duns arrive. Anglers can find success with Hare's Ears below the surface and Sparkle Duns on top. A profusion of caddis come later in August and continue into September, and are followed in the fall by the Tricos. For those willing to brave the vagaries of a Great Plains winter, midges are the order of the day.

If nothing is happening in the way of a hatch, small scuds and San Juan worms can be fished near the bottom with an indicator at almost any time of year and are consistent producers.

For Barry Beck, the Trico hatch continues to captivate. Take the occasion when the Trico-gulping fish wouldn't let him off the river. "Cathy and I were out with Bob Krum, a well-known guide on the river. We were supposed to float down below the Mallard's Landing. We came to the first island and an amazing Trico hatch was coming off. We fished there until two P.M. – we could still see the launch area and realized we had better put some miles on. We started downriver and came to an even larger pod of slurping fish. I'd never seen Tricos on the river past noon, but there they were. Next thing we knew, it was starting to get dark. Somehow, we made it to the take-out where Bob's rig was waiting. It was after eleven. We had Cornish game hens for dinner around two A.M."

The Bighorn has cast a spell on many anglers over the years, luring them away from other lives to set up house near its banks. "There's only one reason in the world that people come to live in Fort Smith, Montana, and that's to be on the 'Horn," Barry said. "I know more than a few guys who've given up marriages and personal possessions to be on the river."

Most visiting anglers focus on the first thirteen miles of the river below the Yellowtail Dam. The crowds, especially in the first three miles below the dam, can be thick, especially in the summertime. The river below Bighorn Access Site slows significantly and the fish populations diminish, drawing far fewer anglers. While the fish are fewer and predominantly browns, they are also bigger. This is a boon for Barry.

DESTINATION

30

133

"There's some very productive water on the lower section, and the fishing is very challenging. The 'Horn is a gentle river at this point, reminiscent of Henry's Fork in places. I like fishing small flies and fine tippets. I can find this kind of angling on the lower Bighorn, and I generally have little competition for the water." Large streamer patterns cast against the banks and stripped quickly to the boat will also generate hard strikes from big brownies in this stretch.

Due to low water conditions in the last few years, fish populations and catch rates on the Bighorn have suffered. But Barry's passion for the river has not dampened. "We haven't seen sensational fishing as of late, but when you fall in love with a river, you stay with it. The river's had some tough times but it's getting better."

OPPOSITE:
An angler
works some
good-looking
water on the
Bighorn.

BARRY BECK and his wife, Cathy, conduct fly-fishing schools, clinics, and presentations and lead fly-fishing trips to fresh- and saltwater destinations around the world. Their photographs appear regularly in sporting calendars and magazines, including *Fly Fisherman* and *Field & Stream* (see www.barryandcathybeck.com). The Becks' books include *Cathy Beck's Fly Fishing Hand-book, Seasons of the Bighorn* (written with George Kelly), *Fly Fishing the Flats,* and *Favorite Pennsylvania Fly Water.*

IF YOU GO

▶ **Prime Time:** Late July through mid-August is when the Bighorn has its most prolific hatches – and accompanying crowds. The river fishes well from early July through September and is also open to fishing in the winter, when despite fiendishly fickle weather it can still fish quite well.

▶ **Getting There:** Fort Smith generally serves as home base for anglers focusing on the Bighorn. The town – a collection of a few fly shops, lodges, and assorted trailers – is about ninety miles southeast of Billings, which is served by a number of commercial carriers. Note that Fort Smith is located on the Crow Indian Reservation. No alcohol is sold there. If you enjoy a drink after fishing you should plan on bringing your own.

▶ **Accommodations:** Fort Smith exists to serve anglers, and a variety of accommodations are available. Kingfisher Lodge (800-835-2529; www.bighornkingfisher.com) offers excellent guides, accommodations, and meals. Simpler accommodations, including rental homes for larger parties, are available from Bighorn Trout Shop (406-666-2375; www.big

DESTINATION

30

135

horntroutshop.com) and Bighorn Fly and Tackle (888-665-1321; www.bighornfly.com); these simpler rooms average $100 per night for two. The fly shops and lodges can arrange guide services (on average, $350 per day for two anglers). It's worthwhile to hire a guide the first day you're out on the river, as he or she can give you a sense of the river's rich entomology. If you have some rowing experience, you can rent a boat the second day and do it yourself.

▶ **Equipment:** As much of the fishing is done from a drift boat, most anglers suit up with with two rods: a 9-foot 4- or 5-weight rig for fishing dries and a 9-foot 6- or 7-weight rod for nymphs and streamers. A floating line will work for all situations except fishing streamers, when you might prefer a sink-tip; reels should carry 100 yards of backing. Bring along 9-foot leaders tapered to 4x or 5x, and tippet from 3x to 7x. Depending on the time of year, the following flies will cover most situations: Parachute Adams, Pheasant Tail, Hare's Ear, Elk Hair Caddis, Stimulators, Sparkle Duns, PMD Cripples, X-Caddis, Parachute Trico, Griffiths Gnat, San Juan Worm, and Scud (check in the local fly shops to see what colors are working). Smaller tends to work better on the Bighorn, so stock up on sizes from #14 to #20 ... and even smaller for the Trico hatch.

RAINBOW TROUT ON
ARMSTRONG'S SPRING CREEK

RECOMMENDED BY **George Anderson**

If rivers were to boast slogans, Armstrong's Spring Creek's would mimic that of the infamous Volkswagen Beetle ad campaign of the 1960s: "Think small."

George Anderson first fished Armstrong's in the mid-sixties, after Joe Brooks recommended it. "I had been fishing the Yellowstone and some of the other bigger rivers in the area a lot, and then I got out on Armstrong's. There were a lot of fish visible in the creek and many hatches coming off simultaneously. It was the first time I ever encountered such selectivity. While there might be Pale Morning Duns and Sulphurs on the surface, the fish would only be feeding on PMD nymphs, then the emergers, then the duns." George learned quickly that one can't get by on Armstrong's with standard patterns. Insect stages have to be properly imitated.

Bubbling up gin-clear just south of the town of Livingston and west of the Yellowstone River, Armstrong's Spring Creek is as beautiful as it is challenging. The creek runs a mile and a half through the meadows and outbuildings of the O'Hair family ranch before it enters the DePuy family ranch, and becomes DePuy Spring Creek. Lined by alders and cottonwoods and shadowed by the twelve-thousand-foot-high Absarokas, the creek averages fifty to one hundred feet in width and three feet in depth, making it easy to wade. Steady water temperatures in the mid-fifties and rich mineral content create undulating beds of water vegetation that provide excellent insect habitat and cover for the fish. While it harbors few monster fish, Armstrong's has healthy numbers of rainbows in the 14- to 20-inch class, as well as some nice browns and cutthroats that run into the stream to spawn.

Years ago, Armstrong's was open to the general public. However, as fly fishing became more popular, more controls were instated to preserve the fishery, first through

Trout Unlimited and then through the landowners. Today, access is limited to twelve anglers a day, and a rod fee of $100 (in the high season) is required. During the peak of the summer hatches in late June and early July, reservations are extremely tough to come by. "These spring creeks would've been wiped out if it wasn't for catch-and-release and paid-fee fishing," George suggested. "The catch-and-release fly-fishing-only regulations on these streams should protect them in perpetuity."

Where the willing cutthroats of the nearby Yellowstone will often offer anglers of modest skill a gentle ego boost, Armstrong's rainbows and browns dispense a cruel lesson in humility. It is not a beginner's stream. The flies cast on Armstrong's are much smaller than what most anglers are accustomed to using. If you're fishing Sulphur patterns, they're size #20s and #22s. Fish might forgive a small variation in color, but the silhouette of the fly is critical.

For newcomers to spring creek fishing, tying on the tiny patterns Armstrong's fish crave – let alone choosing them – can be a study in frustration. For trouting intellectuals, however, the puzzle-solving prospects of Armstrong's promise great delight. "There's no question that it can be tough going out there," George said. "On one occasion recently, there were a bunch of Sulphurs and midges on the water and the fish seemed to be rising to them, but we couldn't figure out what they were taking. Finally, we caught a nice rainbow. Sometimes the best way to solve the puzzle is to go to the source – that is, pump the trout's stomach. We did, and there were no Sulphur duns or adult midges in there, just hundreds of olive midge larvae."

A number of fly patterns have been developed with these spring creeks in mind. George has come up with a few nymph patterns over the years for *Ephemeralla infrequens* – that is, PMDs. His Olive Drake is tied after the style of Polly Rosborough's Gray Drake; it has a darker, more prominent wing case to resemble an emerging mayfly nymph. He also designed a CDC midge emerger, which has been a deadly pattern on the creeks.

Hatches on Armstrong's can be like great jazz pieces – they begin with a basic theme or melody and then spin that melody into myriad improvisations. From January to June, the theme is midges and Blue-Winged Olives; caddis emerge in early June, then give way to PMDs later in the month. Sulphurs appear in mid-July and stay around until late August, when terrestrials appear to provide less seasoned anglers with a fly they can see and understand. In September, Blue-Winged Olives reappear and linger through the fall.

Whatever hatch or microhatch is occurring, it's important to identify one feeding fish

OPPOSITE:
Attention to
"micro-hatches"
is essential for
success on
Armstrong's.

DESTINATION

31

and focus on that fish. Blind-casting – except when prospecting with terrestrials on windy August afternoons – is largely fruitless; fish simply won't move for a presentation that's not exactly in their feeding lane.

"I think the hunting aspect of the Armstrong's fishing experience is one of the reasons it's so popular," George offered. "If there are twenty fish rising, we try to locate the biggest fish by comparing rising forms. Once you identify the biggest fish, then you set up your approach and presentation. You might make fifty to a hundred casts before you find the right combination. Then boom – the fish will take that fly on the first cast. That makes all the effort worthwhile."

GEORGE ANDERSON began his professional fly-fishing career managing a tackle shop in West Yellowstone during college summers. After graduation, he worked for six years with Dan Bailey's Fly Shop, leaving to open the Yellowstone Angler in 1980. George has authored many articles over the years that have appeared in *Fly Fisherman, Trout, Big Sky Journal,* and *Saltwater Fly Fishing.* He has appeared as a guest angler on ESPN's *Fly Fishing the World,* and ESPN2's *Spanish Fly.* George won individual honors at the Jackson Hole One-Fly in the only two years he fished in the event, 1989 and 1990.

IF YOU GO

▶ **Prime Time:** The height of dry-fly fishing comes in late June/early July with the emergence of Brown Drakes and PMDs. This is also the height of the crowds. As Armstrong's is a spring creek with a constant water temperature, it is open year-round and can offer excellent late-season (November) and early-season (March) fishing, with next to no competition. Access is limited to twelve rods a day. Access fees range from $40 per rod in the off-season to $100 per rod in the summer; call 406-222-2979 for reservations. If space is not available on Armstrong's, DePuy Spring Creek (406-222-0221; www.depuyspring creek.com) and Nelson's Spring Creek (406-222-6560) offer similar experiences.

▶ **Getting There:** Armstrong's Spring Creek is just south of the railroad/cowboy/resort town of Livingston, Montana. Bozeman, thirty-five miles to the west, and Billings, 115 miles to the east, are both served by commercial airlines. Armstrong's is less than fifty miles from the northern entrance to Yellowstone National Park.

▶ **Accommodations:** Livingston seems to have successfully made the transition from railroad town to outdoor mecca and offers accommodations ranging from motels to bed and breakfasts. The Blue-Winged Olive (800-471-1141; www.bluewingedolive.net) is a bed and breakfast that caters to anglers and is close to Armstrong's. Chatham's Livingston Bar & Grill (406-222-7909), owned by artist Russell Chatham, offers haute cuisine one might not expect in Livingston.

▶ **Equipment:** Light rods, long leaders, fine tippets, and tiny flies are the rule of thumb on Armstrong's. While one can get by with a 5-weight, a 3- or 4-weight in 8-foot or 9-foot would be better, outfitted with a floating line. You should have 9-foot to 12-foot leaders in 5x and 6x, with tippet material from 1- to 5-pound test. As for flies, it would be wise to visit the Yellowstone Angler (406-222-7130; www.yellowstoneangler.com), just a few miles north of the creek. The staff there has the local intelligence necessary to approach Armstrong's persnickety fish. If you haven't fished spring creeks before – and even if you have – you might do well to retain a guide. Yellowstone Anglers can hook you up with a spring-creek specialist; other guide services include Al Gadoury's 6x Outfitters (406-586-3806) and James Marc (415-302-4224).

DESTINATION

31

RAINBOW TROUT ON
THE UPPER DELAWARE RIVER

RECOMMENDED BY **Paul Weamer**

The Upper Delaware River has been lauded as the best western trout stream in the East. When I asked fly-tying wunderkind Paul Weamer what this meant, he laughed a bit and said, "I'm not sure. We've had guys out from Montana who've said that the Big D is every bit as good as anything they have out there. On a good day, that's probably true. But I think this comparison has come more from the folks who fish the Delaware regularly. They want everyone else to love the Delaware as much as they do."

Nestled in the Catskills and separating New York and Pennsylvania, the Upper Delaware River system comprises more than eighty miles of wild trout water, encompassing the tailwaters of the East Branch and West Branch, and the first twenty-seven miles of the mainstem, to Callicoon, New York. American fly-fishing history runs deep in these waters; it was in the nearby town of Central Valley that rod maker Hiram Leonard set up shop in the early 1880s. Later, fly tier Theodore Gordon ushered in a new era of American fly fishing with his realistic dry-fly creations, which were tested on the Beaverkill, Neversink, and Esopus as well as the Delaware. Where many eastern trout rivers have become history, their fisheries destroyed by the effluence of an ever-infringing population, the Upper Delaware system – with the help of several 1960s-era dams – has thrived. The West Branch of the Delaware hosts healthy populations of brown trout, and fishes well throughout the year; the East Branch sustains browns, rainbows, and brookies and is a great spring and fall fishery; the Big D holds rainbows that average 15 inches and deport themselves like fish half again their size. Such a fishery will turn heads anywhere. It's especially impressive when one considers that it lies within six hours' drive of nearly one fourth of the population of the United States.

While the East and West branches of the Delaware are fine fisheries, it is the Big D

OPPOSITE:
The rainbows
of the Upper
Delaware are
genetically
distinct and
electrifying
on a fly rod.

and its feisty rainbows that captivate many anglers, including Paul Weamer. "The fish in the mainstem are dynamos. A study conducted by Cornell University showed that they're genetically distinct. They're not huge, at least by western standards, but even a fifteen-inch fish will take you into your backing pretty quickly. The mainstem is big water, and these trout know how to work that to their advantage." Rainbow trout are not native to the Delaware, and a favorite explanation of their presence goes like this: in 1885, a train on the old Erie line broke down. Among the train's cargo were several cans of McCloud River-strain rainbows, secured from a downstate hatchery by the train's brakeman, Dan Cahill, who hoped to release the fish near his home on the river's West Branch. Fearing that the fish would expire before the train ever made the forty-five miles to its terminus, Cahill elected to release the fish into nearby Callicoon Creek, an upper Delaware tributary. (New York state records show that there were several scheduled rainbow plantings in the West Branch at roughly the same time, though the Cahill tale is certainly more fanciful.)

From its formation at the Junction Pool in Hancock, New York, the Delaware is a big river, alternating between deep, slow runs and shallow riffles. The hatches on the Big D can be intense, and often confusing, as many bugs may be hatching at once. In springtime, almost every mayfly species that hatches in the eastern United States hatches in the Delaware. "We have many hatches I'd describe as prolific," Paul observed, "but some of the best and most astonishing to witness are the Apple Caddis, Hendrickson, white fly (*Ephoron leukon*), and the Green and Brown Drake spinner falls. The Green Drake hatch can be spectacular. Unfortunately, it's a very brief hatch. If you're not in the region when it comes off, you're probably going to miss it."

Another hatch that Paul is very fond of is the *Isonychia* or Slate Drake. They begin appearing in the spring, trickle off in the summer, and pick up again in the fall. The general rule on the Delaware is that if fish aren't actively feeding on the surface, you won't get much action blind-casting dries. One exception to this rule is the *Isonychia*. Sometimes a cast into the tail of some riffles will bring a big take. Other significant hatches on the Big D include Blue-Winged Olives (throughout the season), Sulphurs (in the summer, when cold water is released from the West Branch), and Tricos (late summer/early fall).

The rainbows of the Upper Delaware are to be treasured, though like most treasures they are not easy to come by. "You're not going to land fifty fish in a day out on the Big D," Paul said. "If you get four or five fish out there, you're having a good day. It can be pretty technical fishing – long leaders, light tippets, and tiny flies, not to mention complex hatches. The Delaware is a great, great test. Friends of mine who have fished all over the world put the river on their list of the top two or three toughest rivers that they've ever fished. And they keep coming back."

PAUL WEAMER is a writer, lecturer, fly-fishing guide, and the managing partner of the Ultimate Flyfishing Store located in Hancock, New York. He spent four years working as a counselor in both residential facilities and public schools before going to work managing a fly-fishing lodge on the Delaware. He has been a production fly tier for numerous guides and shops in the Catskill Mountains and his flies have been featured in many periodicals and in the Catskill Fly Fishing Museum. He is a member of the pro staffs of both Hobie Sunglasses and Daiichi hooks, where he designed the Daiichi #1230, Weamer's Truform™ Mayfly Hook.

IF YOU GO

▶ **Prime Time:** Late spring has the greatest concentration of hatches on the Big D. One of Paul's favorite hatches, the *Isonychia*, occurs in both spring and fall.

▶ **Getting There:** The town of Hancock, New York, makes a great Upper Delaware base. It's within three hours of New York City and Philadelphia, four and a half hours from Washington, D.C., and six hours from Boston.

▶ **Accommodations:** Smith's Colonial Motel (607-637-2989) and Green Acres Motel (607-467-3620) offer basic accommodations. Al Caucci's Delaware Fishing Club (800-6MAYFLY; www.mayfly.com) offers a resort setting on the Pennsylvania side of the river. West Branch Angler Resort (607-467-5525; www.westbranchangler.com) offers another resort setting upstream on the West Branch of the Delaware.

▶ **Equipment:** A 9-foot, 5- or 6-weight rod equipped with floating line and 100 yards of backing should give you what you need to stop the Big D's hard-driving rainbows. Hatches are quite varied, but anglers will do well to stock Tricos (#24), Blue-Winged Olives (#14-#24), Sulfur Dun (#14), Dun Variant (#12), Green and Brown Drakes (#12-#14), and White Flies (#12-#14). The Ultimate Flyfishing Store in Hancock (607-637-4296) provides fishing reports and guide services.

BROWN AND RAINBOW TROUT

ON THE SOUTH ISLAND

RECOMMENDED BY **Chris Daughters**

The South Island of New Zealand is awash in beauty and teeming with trout. A mountain range, the Southern Alps, stretches almost the length of the island, punctuating the sky with peaks reaching thirteen thousand feet. The western edge of the island is quite moist, reminiscent of the coastal areas of the Pacific Northwest. The mountain regions are lush, and the drier country east of the mountains produces vast amounts of wool. The trout of New Zealand – browns and rainbows that average nearly 3 pounds, with many fish in the 6- to 8-pound class – are descendants of turn-of-the-century transplants. With little competition from indigenous species, they have thrived. Today, these intruders are considered as natural a part of the landscape as sheep ... another Kiwi émigré.

The South Island trouting experience is certainly one of quality rather than quantity. A majority of the rivers simply don't support large numbers of fish. Some of the most fishy-looking water you can imagine may not contain a single fish. Despite this, resourceful anglers can go it on their own in New Zealand, if they're willing to ask a few questions and allot some extra time to account for hit-and-miss explorations. That's how Chris Daughters first fished New Zealand ten years ago. "I was still in school when I first visited the South Island. I had heard it was a great place to go for a fishing vacation on the cheap. Some guys from the fly shop and I saved our pennies all summer, and spent three months that winter bumming around. I feel that South Island fishing is quite conducive to getting in the car with a guidebook and checking things out. While things are spread out, you can get just about anywhere in a day. You look at the weather report in the morning, and then decide where you want to go."

During subsequent visits, Chris has used the central island towns of Kurow and Omarama as a base. One of the South Island's major rivers, the Waitaki, flows through

OPPOSITE:
It's not too
difficult to find
solitude on
the beautiful
streams of the
South Island.

DESTINATION

33

Kurow and offers both excellent fishing and easy access. Unlike many Southland rivers, the Waitaki boasts prolific hatches – specifically, caddis – through much of the season. "Most of the fish are two to five pounds, but it also gets some bigger migratory fish," Chris said. "Some of the tributaries of the Waitaki fish well too."

There are too many noteworthy rivers and lakes on the South Island to list here. The Eglinton, Wilkin, Manapouri, Dingleburn, and Ahuriri are known for their beauty and fine fishing, but many lesser-known streams can reward the patient and skilled angler with trophy trout. Local residents are shockingly unsecretive about the fishing. If you stop at one of the combination pub/hotel/gas station establishments that dot most towns, people are invariably generous with angling information. "You get the sense that trout are no big thing to many Kiwis," Chris opined. "The farmers' attitude is 'You want fish, they're out in my backyard.' People are conscious that tourism is a big part of their country's economy and identity. Maintaining a sense of nicety is important to them. For a lot of the fishing you do on your own, you'll need to pass through private property. Getting permission is no problem at all. In fact, there have been a number of occasions when landowners would invite me in for a drink or offer to show me the farm. Once you begin asking around, they'll refer you to their friends, and they'll invite you to come over and fish from their property."

It's worth noting that "fishing" on the South Island is closely equated with "walking." As mentioned above, fish are often few and far between, and you will generally need to cover some water – miles of water – to locate fish. This is where New Zealand's much-heralded sight-fishing technique comes most into play. On many rivers it's smarter to assume that if you don't see a fish, there aren't any fish, and move along until you find one. Blind-casting, especially on the smaller gin-clear streams one might encounter off the beaten path, is a lower-percentage game. (South Island guide Ben Kemp estimates that 60 to 70 percent of the fish caught are spotted first.) Not to say that sight-fishing here is easy.

The trout – even big fish in the 25-inch range – blend into their environs incredibly well. The successful sight-fisher needs to be attuned to the subtlest movement – the flash of a fish turning to take a nymph, a shadow over a rock. It's a very steep learning curve, one that you'll climb a bit faster with the help of a guide. Many do-it-yourselfers will retain a guide for at least one or two outings, just to get the sense of fish spotting. There are anglers who never quite get the feel for locating New Zealand trout, spying fish only when they actually rise to their fly, or when their guide instructs them to set the hook as a trout slurps the nymph. Good teamwork between guide and angler is essential in these situations; performed correctly, the spotting/casting/setting dance can be a graceful *pas de deux*. Some visitors never spot trout because their streamside approach is, well, lacking in subtlety. If the fish sees you, odds are good that you'll never see it! A low profile and a measured and focused assault are important in most fishing situations, no more so than in the Southland.

An angling trip to the South Island is not complete without at least one backcountry adventure. A helicopter or bush plane will spirit you over the mountains and into a valley of beech forests and emerald-green rivers. You'll surreptitiously hike the river, taking cues from your guide. If you come upon a finning rainbow you'll present a dry first, and if that's ignored you'll follow with a nymph. If you (or, more likely, your guide) spot a holding brown, you'll cast upstream with a nymph. Maybe, just maybe, he'll take.

"You're not going to catch a million fish on the South Island," Chris mused, "but you will remember the fish you catch. You have to take the time to approach the pool and really think about what you're doing. If you're willing to walk a bit, you'll likely have water to yourself."

CHRIS DAUGHTERS grew up fishing Oregon's McKenzie and Willamette rivers. He took up fly fishing at age ten, taking classes at the Caddis Fly Shop in Eugene. He put himself through college working at the shop and guiding; in 1996, he purchased the shop. Chris still guides more than a hundred days a year. When he's not working, he continues to travel and chase fish of all species, with particular interest in saltwater flats and remote trout-fishing destinations.

IF YOU GO

▶ **Prime Time:** New Zealand's summer season is opposite ours here in the Northern Hemisphere, and that's the best time to be there – namely, mid-November to December and mid-January to March.

▶ **Getting There:** The South Island's principal cities – Christchurch and Queenstown – are both served by Air New Zealand (800-262-1234; www.airnz.co.nz). From there, you'll need to rent a car to begin your explorations. (Travelers planning on spending a month or more will sometimes buy a used car and sell it upon their departure.) *Trout Fishing in Southland New Zealand,* published by the Southland Fish and Game Council (+64 32 14 45 01), is a valuable guide for visitors.

▶ **Accommodations:** Many anglers doing it themselves on the South Island will camp in holiday parks (e.g., campgrounds) or stay in rooms provided by publicans. The New Zealand Tourism Commission (www.purenz.com) has a list of all accommodations available. If you prefer a lodge setting, Cedar Lodge (+64 34 43 82 84; www.cedarlodge.net) is considered the island's finest. Guests enjoy daily fly-outs to backcountry waters, superb guides, and access to fishing in Mount Aspiring National Park. Seven-night/six-day all-inclusive packages run $4,345 with double occupancy and shared guide; limited to six anglers at a time.

▶ **Equipment:** A 9-foot, 5- or 6-weight rod equipped with floating line and 100 yards of backing will give you enough muscle for most situations. A neutral-colored fly line will spook fewer trout than fluorescent line; 9- to 12-foot leaders tapered to 3x to 4x and tippet material in 4- to 8-pound test will satisfy terminal tackle needs. Standard U.S. trout flies will work fine, as fish tend to be opportunistic rather than focusing on particular hatches. For dries, bring Adams, Elk Hair Caddis, Green Beetles, Royal Wulffs, Humpies, and Joe's Hoppers in #12 to #16. For nymphs, bring Pheasant Tails, Hare's Ears, and Copper Johns in #12 to #16. An abundance of good information regarding fisheries and guides is available online. A few worthwhile sites include www.fly-fishing-guides-new-zealand.co.nz and www.flyfishingnz.co.nz.

NORTHERN PIKE ON

GREAT SLAVE LAKE

RECOMMENDED BY **Steve Probasco**

Northern pike (*Esox lucius*) generally do not occupy a respected spot in the pantheon of fly anglers' most-sought-after species. Dubbed "water wolves," "freshwater barracudas," and other unflattering sobriquets, these unrelenting predators can be an impediment to the successful pursuit of other game fish that cohabit their environs, intercepting flies before they can reach their intended target. Worse yet, their illicit introduction into river systems can threaten the very existence of salmonid species, which fall prey to the pike's voracious appetite.

For a moment, however, let us consider the pike in a more favorable light – more specifically, the northern lights of the Northwest Territory. Steve Probasco has plied the most storied steelhead and trout rivers of the West for all of his life, yet when asked about an extraordinary fly-fishing experience, questing for trophy pike on the North Arm of Great Slave Lake came to mind. "People think of pike as a deepwater species. This is often true, especially for the larger fish. However, when the ice begins to break up – which is usually in early June on Great Slave Lake – the big fish move into shallow water. I've fished to four-foot-long northerns in as little as two feet of water. When a fish that size smashes a surface popper, you're talking about some exciting angling."

Great Slave Lake is North America's fifth-largest lake, running three hundred miles in length and covering nearly eleven thousand square miles. It's named for the Slave Indians and rests along the Northwest Territory's southwestern border with Alberta. The Hay and Slave rivers are its chief tributaries, providing a rich food source for the baitfish that in turn feed the lake's gargantuan pike. The northerns here grow to up to 50 inches and 40 pounds. The surroundings of granite and dark spruce forests are somewhat austere, and the weather – even in early June – can be capricious, with snow a possibility. All

that being said, there's simply no better place to pursue giant pike with a fly rod.

While Great Slave Lake reaches depths of 2,015 feet, its northern arm contains many shallows. Large fish from throughout the lake system move into the North Arm to spawn as the water warms, making for incredible sport. The lake's water is crystal clear; sight-fishing is the order of the day. All angling is conducted from a boat. Anglers cruise along the shoreline, patrolling little bays and inlets until a large fish is spotted. "You stand up in the boat almost like you're fishing the flats for bonefish," Steve said. "If we don't see big fish – and I'm defining big as pike in the forty-five- to fifty-inch class – we'll go elsewhere. On one occasion, we cruised into a bay that looked as though it were covered with large logs. I threw a cast out and one of the logs moved and took the fly. I make sure to fish that bay whenever I visit, as the pike tend to return to the same spawning grounds each spring."

There's not a great deal of subtlety involved in the pursuit of pike. Your goal is to get a fly in front of the fish – either a popping bug or a big streamer will generally do – and strip it back. If you find a fish and get the fly in front of it, odds are very good the pike will hit it – even inches from the boat! Then the fun really starts. Pike are the fastest freshwater fish, capable of short bursts of speed up to thirty-five miles per hour. A 45-inch northern will put a dangerous bend in an 8-weight rod and can "customize" your favorite two-piece into a three-piece if you're not careful. While pike aren't known for their blistering long runs, they are none too eager to come to the boat. If you hook up with a big fish, expect to play it awhile.

Trout Rock Wilderness Lodge espouses catch-and-release angling for its trophy pike. Anglers, however, are encouraged to kill a smaller fish for a lunchtime treat. The guides here delight in preparing a shore lunch of fried pike, which seems a just reward for a visitor who's spent the morning hucking large flies and battling lunch's larger brethren.

STEVE PROBASCO has been fly fishing the rivers of the western United States for most of his fifty years. He's the author of several books on fly fishing, including *Yakima River Journal, Montana Blue Ribbon Fly Fishing Guide,* and *Probasco's Favorite Northwest Flies.* He resides near Washington's Olympic Peninsula and currently edits two publications, *Northwest Fly Fishing* and *Southwest Fly Fishing* (www.nwflyfishing.net).

OPPOSITE:
In early June, gargantuan pike move into the shallows of Great Slave Lake to spawn, providing some fast and furious fly-rod action.

DESTINATION

34

IF YOU GO

▶ **Prime Time:** The first two weeks after ice-out, which generally occurs in early June, are best. While some good fishing can be had through September, the bigger fish move to deeper water, making them a less accessible target for fly rodders.

▶ **Getting There:** The staging point for the North Arm of Great Slave Lake is Yellow-knife, the burgeoning capital (population: 18,000) of Northwest Territories. Yellowknife can be reached by jet from many U.S. cities, as well as from major Canadian cities.

▶ **Accommodations:** On the North Arm, there's one game in town: Trout Rock Wilderness Lodge (867-873-4334; www.enodah.com). The lodge provides boats, guides, and all of your meals. The guides, who are members of the Yellowknife Dene First Nation, know the lake extremely well, and understand the special needs of fly fishers seeking northerns. All-inclusive packages for three days/three nights are $1,295 per person.

▶ **Equipment:** A 9-foot rod in the 8- to 9-weight range will do the trick. Weight-forward floating lines will suffice for most situations. The pike are not leader shy; use 20- to 30-pound test with 20-pound test wire tippets, so you don't lose your trophy to a northern's wolflike teeth. Nor are pike particularly picky about what they eat. Almost any large streamer pattern (such as a Clouser Minnow or Bunny Leech) or popper will produce; flies should be tied on heavy wire hooks in size #2/0 to #4/0. More than anything else, flies should be durable; those teeth are tough on feathers and fur. Be sure to have jaw spreaders handy to facilitate safe release of fish.

ATLANTIC SALMON ON

THE ALTA RIVER

RECOMMENDED BY **Mike Fitzgerald, Sr.**

The rugged, glacier-forged landmass of Norway is riddled with icy streams, streams brimming with Atlantic salmon. More than six hundred Norwegian rivers hold fishable populations of salmon. In the far north, three hundred miles above the perimeter of the Arctic Circle, runs the king of all Atlantic salmon rivers, the Alta. The Alta is the world's most prolific producer of large salmon; there's no other venue that offers anglers a bet-ter chance of taking a fish in the 40- or 50-pound class. Not surprisingly, this character-istic has made the Alta the most exclusive salmon fishery in the world.

The Alta runs seventy miles due north from the high plateaus of central Finnmark to the sea at Altafjord. The environs of the river are varied, though all are spectacular. Pastoral meadows and farmland in the lower river give way to steep cliffs and waterfalls. By the time one reaches the famous royal beats upriver at Sautso, the Alta's glacier-fed water cuts through the deepest canyon in Europe. It can be a large and intimidating river in places, but the beats provide some superb fly-fishing water.

While the Vikings of Norway were quite adept at vanquishing other nation-states, the Alta was conquered, at least in part, by the English. Aristocratic sportsmen seeking new waters arrived at Altafjord in the 1830s and had their boats poled through the lower river's great rapids by their crews. The size of the river's salmon was as impressive then as it is now. The duke of Roxborough's family has been fishing the Alta since the 1850s, as have the progeny of the duke of Westminster. One of the dukes of Westminster holds a hallowed place in the annals of Alta angling – thirty-three fish landed on one evening in July in 1926. More than eight hundred pounds of salmon came to the beach that fate-ful night, including one fish of 42 pounds.

To fish the fabled pools of the Alta, anglers may wait decades – or a lifetime. Some of

the best beats are in the hands of English and Norwegian nobility, and they are passed from generation to generation. Other beats may become available only upon the passing of their holder. When a spot does become open, there's a long line of prospects waiting to pay the $10,000 to $12,000 it costs to lease a rod for a week. Even Mike Fitzgerald, a gentleman with some connections in the fly-fishing world, had to wait fifteen years. "I started thinking about the Alta in 1971. The catch reports, both in terms of numbers and size of fish, were just mind-boggling. I wanted to experience it at least once. In 1986, the opportunity finally arose. I've been back every year since."

Fishing on the Alta takes place between eight P.M. and four A.M., when the twenty-four-hour light in June and July is at its lowest level. Techniques are determined by water level and temperature. Higher, colder water is the norm in the earlier season, and most anglers use large tube flies with intermediate sinking or sink-tip lines to reach the fish. In July and August, floating lines and smaller flies can generate good results. Fish seem to like the fly on a slightly faster swing; not much line mending is necessary. The fish are uninterested in skated dry flies. "Even when you're fishing intermediate lines," Mike recalled, "the takes are quite visible. The fish are that big." Much of the fishing is done from twenty-eight-foot canoes hewn from Norwegian pine. The canoes are rowed and paddled by local boatsmen with generations of experience. "The boatsmen are very smooth," Mike said. "They make very precise drops without using anchors, and they have excellent knowledge of where the fish will be holding at various water levels." While making it easier to reach the fish, canoes also make it easier to land fish quickly, so they're not overstressed.

"The lore of a river like the Alta is a great part of the experience," Mike opined. "There are boatsmen whose families have worked on the river for four, five, seven generations. They'll share stories of how their grandfather or great-grandfather guided the king while we're enjoying our midnight lunch around a fire. Fishing on the river has been documented since the late 1700s. You feel a very tangible sense of history and tradition when you are there."

The largest salmon on the Alta's record books is 64 pounds. There are tales of other mammoth fish, estimated at 60 or 70 pounds, which have been fought for hours, followed miles downstream, and lost. Mike's best fish on the Alta was 43 pounds; he's seen fish of up to 55 pounds caught. His most memorable fish, however, were the first Alta salmon caught by his children. "My daughter's fish came to a rather eclectic tube fly that

*OPPOSITE:
The Alta's
best angling
generally
occurs between
eight P.M. and
four A.M. –
the lowest-
light periods
in the early
summer.*

DESTINATION

35

our guide chose. There was a huge boil, as if the bottom of the river had risen up a foot. The fish ran straight upstream for a hundred yards and went around a rock. Seconds later, the fish jumped a hundred yards downstream, even though the line was still heading upstream. Our boatsman quickly rowed up to the rock and plucked the line clear. Then the chase began. Mollie's first Alta salmon was thirty-five pounds."

Some who have the good fortune to wade the Alta have royal blood pumping through their veins. Yet once you make it on the river, such distinctions fall away. "Salmon fishing is a great equalizer," Mike mused. "As you're working through a pool, the lot you've been cast in life means less than how well you cast. That's how the fish feel. And I think that's how most sportsmen feel, too."

MIKE FITZGERALD, SR., founded Frontiers International Travel with his wife, Susie, in 1969 and has served as president and chief executive officer of the company for the past thirty-four years. He was involved in the early development of a number of fly-fishing destinations that remain mainline Frontiers programs today. These include flats fishing on Mexico's Yucatán Peninsula, Christmas Island, the Ponoi River in Russia, shooting and fishing in Argentina, and fishing in both Iceland and the Alta River in Norway. His travels have included fifty-three countries on five continents. He has served on various boards of directors, including the Atlantic Salmon Federation and the American Museum of Fly Fishing.

DESTINATION

35

IF YOU GO

▶ **Prime Time:** Anytime you can get a spot! The Alta season runs from June through August; the most productive time on the river is generally considered mid-June to mid-July, though August can be good as well. The bottom line is that spots on the river are so rare that if one presents itself you should grab it. Frontiers (800-245-1950; www.frontiers travel.com) maintains a list of anglers who wish to fish the Alta, and every few years ad hoc opportunities do become available. Norway Salmon Fishing (www.salmonfish ing.no) can provide information regarding the lottery system for the lower river and help you locate a beat on one of Norway's other fine salmon rivers, like the Tana, the Malselv, or the Gaula.

► **Getting There:** You'll want to fly into the town of Alta, which is served by SAS (800-221-2350; www.scandinavian.net) from Oslo. Several carriers provide service from the United States to Oslo, Norway, including SAS and Iceland Air (800-223-5500; www.ice landair.com).

► **Accommodations:** If you're able to secure a spot on the Alta, lodge accommodation is generally provided. If you go it on your own or just wish to visit, a couple of hotel options include Nordlys Hotel Alta (+47 78 45 72 00) and Rica Hotel Alta (+47 78 48 27 00; www.rica.no).

► **Equipment:** Spey rods in 8- or 9-weight are preferred on larger Norwegian rivers like the Alta. Bring floating, intermediate sinking, and sink-tips lines, with 250 yards of backing, in case you hook into one of those 50-pounders! Nine-foot leaders tapered to 0x with 10- to 16-pound tippet work best. Early in the season, anglers rely on larger tube flies. When the water warms and river levels lower, traditional patterns in smaller sizes work well.

STEELHEAD ON THE
NORTH UMPQUA RIVER

RECOMMENDED BY **Frank Moore**

The steelhead of the North Umpqua first came to notoriety from the dispatches of west-ern novelist Zane Grey for *Sports Afield* and other outdoor magazines in the thirties. At this time, fly fishing for steelhead was in its nascent stages; sophisticated shooting heads and sinking lines were decades away. At first, fly anglers relied on level, then double-taper floating lines and dry or standard wet flies to find their quarry. A number of popu-lar steelhead patterns were developed on the North Umpqua, including the Skunk (cre-ated by Mildred Krogel), the Umpqua Special, the Cummings, and the Black Gordon.

Today, many who fish the North Umpqua still favor floating lines and surface-orient-ed patterns. In fact, regulations now forbid the use of weighted flies on the North Umpqua's thirty-one miles of fly-fishing-only water. The two thousand to three thousand wild fish that enter the river from June through September are not particularly large – averaging 8 to 10 pounds – but they are strong enough to send an angler scrambling hundreds of yards downstream in their pursuit. (A few fish each year do eclipse 20 pounds.) The fish are generally skittish, finning near the bottom and feeding infre-quently. There's much debate as to why steelhead will strike a fly. While it's been shown that the fish will sometimes feed on insects upon entering the river, many believe that a steelhead strikes a fly from an aggressive territorial instinct. In steelheading circles, this point has been debated over many fifths of scotch well into the night. Everyone agrees that your odds of hooking up greatly improve when you get your fly in the water, as Frank Moore can attest.

"The first thing I ever caught on the North Umpqua was a wooden bridge that used to span Steamboat Creek at the Camp Waters, back in 1946. I was riding in a pickup truck with a friend from Roseburg. The fly came loose from the rod and attached to the

OPPOSITE:
It takes
long casts to
effectively
cover the
fabled pools
of the North
Umpqua.

DESTINATION

36

bridge. The bridge put up a great fight – took out all my line and most of my backing before we stopped the truck."

Where some steelhead rivers are renowned for a certain type of holding water, the North Umpqua offers just about any type of steelhead water you could care to fish – runs, pools, pocket water, and everything in between. Wherever you choose to cast a line, you can bet that wading will be tricky. Slippery footing, fast currents, and clear water that complicates depth perception make each step mildly treacherous. Oregon angling writer John Shewey wrote in *Oregon Blue-Ribbon Fly Fishing Guide* that when wading the North Umpqua, "one ought to just sit down in the river first thing in the morning just to get the dunking over with."

In the time since Zane Grey's articles, presidents and potentates have plied the North Umpqua's waters. Jimmy Carter has fished the North Umpqua; rumors have it that the noble former president had no luck. Some anglers frown on the well-mannered mien of the North Umpqua, where sinking lines are discouraged and a streamside etiquette of sharing pools is informally enforced. This gentle anachronism is refreshing in a time of increased fishing pressure and decreasing courtesy.

Nowhere on the river is this old-fashioned sense of propriety more in place than the pools of the Camp Water, a half-mile stretch that steelhead guru Trey Combs has called "the most celebrated water in all of steelhead fly fishing." The stretch begins at Mott Bridge and includes at least sixteen discrete segments of holding water – Bridge Hole, Sawtooth, Hayden's Run, Sweetheart, Confluence Hole, Station Hole, Upper Boat, Middle Boat, Lower Boat, Kitchen Hole, Fighting Hole, Upper Mott, Middle Mott, Lower Mott, Glory Hole, and Gordon. A few of the spots – Sweetheart and Confluence, for example – demand a precarious cross-river wade. Others, like the Kitchen Hole, require a tightrope walk upon a ledge to reach the casting station that will allow the intrepid angler to get the proper drift; a detour off the ledge, and you're swimming.

Steelhead fly-fishing success is not measured in fish per day but in days per fish – going can be that hard. The North's tricky currents and uncertain wading make good fly presentation quite challenging, often requiring casts of seventy feet or more, the kind of cast that's beyond the ability of many anglers. But the reward of getting a steelhead to take a fly that's skated along the surface makes the travails worthwhile. "It's something to see them come up and take a free-floating fly or a skater," Frank said. "Sometimes they'll just suck it under. Other times, they'll come three or four feet out of the air and take the fly coming down. Over my many years on the river, I've had superb luck with a number eight Muddler. I don't trim the deer hair on the head very much – I call it an Ugly Muddler. Maybe it's the way the current teases the hairs, but who can tell? I think much of the time the angler is a lot more choosy than the fish."

One of the longest moments in fly fishing is the time between the take of a steelhead and the setting of the hook. The idea is to let the fish take the fly, return to its lie, and thus hook itself. By setting the hook at the moment of contact, the angler essentially kills the deal by pulling the fly out of the fish's mouth. Anglers who can overcome the urge to set the hook when a steelhead takes a surface fly will hook more fish. Frank commented on the North Umpqua's long allure for anglers. "I think many consider the North Umpqua to be the finishing school for steelhead fly fishing. Normally, you have to be a halfway decent fly fisher to consistently hook a fish here. If you think you're good and want to improve, you can do so here on one of the most beautiful rivers around."

A late summer's day on the North Umpqua will have many casts, a few unintended swims, a banged shin or two, and probably no fish. Fortunately, a rich reward awaits successful and nonsuccessful anglers alike at the Steamboat Inn. Over the years, the Steamboat Inn has catered to thousands of anglers with its celebrated "fisherman's suppers," which are in reality gourmet dinners, served conveniently late to maximize fishing time. At eight P.M. a bell tolls, summoning dinner guests to the "The Library," a graciously appointed room that overlooks the river. Here, homemade hors d'oeuvres and locally made Pinot Gris and Pinot Noir are served, usually accompanied by a generous helping of fish stories. At nine, guests are summoned to the dining room for a family-style feast on entrées ranging from medallions of lamb to prime rib to salmon. It's a wonderfully civilized way to end the day. And usually there's at least one success story promising enough to fortify you for another day's humbling.

DESTINATION

36

FRANK MOORE began guiding on the North Umpqua more than fifty years ago and has led many dignitaries to the river's fabled pools. He and his wife built and operated the Steamboat Inn, which has catered to steelheaders since the late 1950s. He served two terms on the Oregon Fish and Wildlife Commission and was a member of the National Parks angling advisory group. Frank has received the National Wildlife Federation–Sears Roebuck Foundation Conservationist of the Year Award, the Izaak Walton League Beaver Award for conservation achievement, and the Anders Award for wild trout management.

In 2003 he was awarded the Federation of Fly Fishers' (F F F) Conservation Award for his good work.

IF YOU GO

▶ **Prime Time:** Summer steelhead generally begin arriving in the North Umpqua's fly-fishing water in good numbers by late July. While conditions vary year to year, mid-August through September is generally the best time to be on the river.

▶ **Getting There:** The North Umpqua's fly-fishing waters begin roughly twenty miles from the town of Roseburg, Oregon, about 225 miles southeast of Portland. Commercial air service is available into Medford and Eugene – both about 120 miles from Steamboat – as well as Portland.

▶ **Accommodations:** Steamboat Inn (800-840-8825; www.thesteamboatinn.com) offers rustic elegance and close proximity to some of the North Umpqua's most storied pools. The Dogwood Motel (541-496-3403) offers more modest digs, also convenient to the river. Numerous campgrounds are also available.

▶ **Equipment:** A 9-foot rod in 7- or 8-weight outfitted with a floating line and at least 150 yards of backing will be adequate for most situations; Spey rods can be useful in covering some of the pools in the Camp Water. A 9-foot leader tapered to 1x is recommended, with tippets from 6- to 10-pound test. Popular waking patterns include Steelhead Caddis, Bombers, or Muddler Minnows in #2 through #6. If skaters aren't moving the fish, tie on a Green Butt Skunk. Access to good water is easy, but fishing it effectively can be challenging for first-time visitors. A guide can help you make the most of your time on the river. Two possibilities are River Wolf Guide Service (541-496-0326) and Summer Run Fly Guides (541-496-3037). The folks at the Steamboat Inn can suggest others.

DESTINATION

36

REDSIDES AND STEELHEAD ON
THE DESCHUTES RIVER

RECOMMENDED BY **Mark Bachmann**

The Deschutes River slices through the center of Oregon, flowing some three hundred miles north from its humble beginnings at Little Lava Lake in the Cascade Mountains to its terminus at the Columbia River. In the lower hundred miles from Pelton Dam to the Columbia, the Deschutes is a powerful, imposing river. The rugged, two-thousand-foot-tall basalt canyons and high desert environs that envelop the Deschutes augment its beauty; a river of such fecundity seems misplaced amid the stark, sagebrush surroundings, a veritable oasis.

The oasis of the Deschutes offers anglers a double bonanza – wild rainbow trout and summer steelhead. "The Deschutes is a singular rarity in that it supports a prolific endemic wild trout population as well as the best floating-line steelhead fishery in the lower forty-eight," said Mark Bachmann, who's fished the Deschutes since the early seventies. "During the fall, an angler can chase steelhead in the morning and evening, and fish for redsides during the day. Not a bad combination!"

Deschutes redsides are a subspecies of rainbow trout called "desert red band trout" or *Oncorhynchus mykiss irideus*. They average between 13 inches and 18 inches, with some larger fish to 24 inches landed each year. While not extremely large by some western river standards, these fish are broad-shouldered, extremely strong, and know how to get the most from the Deschutes' powerful currents. Many Deschutes anglers will recount occasions when they've hooked a 26-inch fish, battled it for fifteen minutes, and finally brought it to hand, only to find that they've actually been fighting a 15-inch redside.

The rich biomass of the Deschutes provides well for its residents. "The Deschutes has a pH level of eight, which makes it one of the most prolific insect generators you can imagine," Mark continued. "It's a bug factory." Caddis make up a significant part of the

DESTINATION

37

165

redside diet through much of the year, and patterns mimicking various stages of their life cycle – Beadhead Pheasant Tails for nymphal stages, soft hackles for emergers, and Elk Hair Caddis for adults – are standard fare. Stoneflies also make up a significant part of the trout's diet. If the fish won't move for dries or smaller nymphs, a Kaufmann's Stonefly fished close to the bottom will often stir up some action. Don't ignore pockets close to shore; the redsides are seeking cover from the river's rapid flow just like you are.

The stoneflies lead to an annual frenzy in the upper sixty miles of the lower Deschutes – the salmonfly hatch. From mid-May to mid-June, these orange bundles of protein emerge from the river and crawl up the branches of riverside cottonwoods and alders. When the wind blows, fish move under the trees and slurp away. Action doesn't generally last through the day, as it doesn't take too many of these bugs to satiate the fish. If you catch it right, however, it makes for a memorable morning.

While the redside fishery alone is enough to merit the Deschutes' special status among western rivers, it is the steelhead runs that bring anglers in droves. "Deschutes steelhead are very aggressive and inclined to take flies near the surface," Mark said. "I believe this occurs because of the size of the river, the water temperature, its coloration, and the shade the canyon provides. You have all the factors for a good surface-oriented fishery working in your favor on the Deschutes."

The Deschutes offers summer steelheaders a particularly long season of fresh incoming fish. Three distinct runs enter the river. A run of hatchery-bred fish generally commences in early July and is made up of fish averaging 6 to 12 pounds. They are followed by a wild run of fish – the "A" run – that enters the river in later July and August and is composed of smaller fish in the 4- to 6-pound class. From September through November, another run of wild fish (the "B" run) enters the river, and this is composed of fish weighing from 10 to 16 pounds. Because the Deschutes runs several degrees cooler than the Columbia, many steelhead aiming for upper Columbia tributaries take up temporary residence in the river, adding to the fun.

"The Deschutes is a premium waking fly river," Mark offered. "Though I believe the most reliable way to catch fish is to fish a darker, wet fly just below the surface." The Deschutes has spawned a number of hair-wing patterns, including the Mack's Canyon, the Street Walker, and the Freight Train.

A key to success is finding water where steelhead are likely to rest and where you can present your fly at the right speed. Ideally, water should be moving at the speed of a slow

OPPOSITE:
The Deschutes
is a fecund oasis
slicing through
central Oregon's
austere high
desert country.

DESTINATION

37

walk, be 3 to 6 feet deep, and include structure, such as boulders or ledges. Deschutes anglers deploy the classic dry-line steelhead approach: cast across and slightly downstream, throw a mend in the line to slow the fly down, and let the fly swing down below you. You'll want to keep a loop of line in your hand, as the fish will often grab the fly gently on the swing and swim back to its lie with the fly in its mouth. If you set the hook prematurely, you'll pull the fly away. When the fish feels the steel, it will often set the hook itself. Then all hell breaks loose. "I've had fish take me three-tenths of a mile down the river," Mark reminisced. "Keeping up with a hot fish like that on the slippery basalt is no small feat!"

A certain magic descends upon the Deschutes in early fall, when the sun dips just below the top of the rimrock canyons, casting shade across the green waters. Anglers rise from their siestas to congregate at the reliable runs above Mack's Canyon, throwing successively longer casts down and across, down and across. Sometimes, as one of the Union Pacific freight trains chugs by on the tracks that parallel the river on the western bank, you'll hear the *click-click-click* of line slowly leaving the reel. When the clicks accelerate into a scream, it is as though the angler has hooked into the train itself.

MARK BACHMANN has been catching steelhead with flies since 1963 and now is part owner of the Fly Fishing Shop in Welches, Oregon. He also guides steelhead anglers eighty-plus days a year on the Sandy River and the Deschutes. A Federation of Fly Fishers (FFF) certified fly-casting instructor, Mark is the author of the *Sandy River Steelhead Journal*, and has worked tirelessly to preserve the Sandy River watershed.

IF YOU GO

▶ **Prime Time:** Prime steelhead season is August through October. Redsides fish well from mid-May through June and then again in the early fall.

▶ **Getting There:** Maupin and Madras, Oregon, are both roughly two hours from the Portland International Airport. While many anglers float the Deschutes to cover the most possible water, a bumpy (though passable) access road gives landlocked anglers entry to more than thirty miles of the river.

▶ **Accommodations:** The towns of Maupin and Madras generally serve as headquarters for Deschutes trips. Several reasonably priced motels are available in each town. Maupin

DESTINATION

37

options include the Deschutes Motel (541-395-2626) and Imperial Lodge (541-395-2404). Madras options include Relax Inn (541-475-2117) and Royal Dutch Motel (541-475-2281). Some outfitters conduct multiday float trips on the river; camping out is a wonderful option – it gives you first crack at good steelhead runs at first light on your "camp water."

▶ **Equipment**: A spey outfit in a 7- or 8-weight (13-foot or 14-foot) allows you to throw a long line with less fatigue, even in areas where there's limited back-casting room. A floating line and 150 yards of backing, with a 9-foot leader tapered to 1x and tippets from 6- to 10-pound test will work for most situations. Sink-tips can be handy later in the season. Proven patterns include Mack's Canyon, Freight Train, Street Walker, and the Fly DuJour, in #4 to #6; for waking patterns, bring Afterdinner Mints, Muddler Minnows, and Steelhead Caddis, in #4 to #6. For trout angling, a 9-foot 5-weight outfitted with floating line is ideal, with 9-foot tapered leaders in 4x or 5x and tippet from 3- to 6-pound. Hatches vary greatly with the season – consult a local fly shop before visiting. Three good guides are Mark Bachmann (800-266-3971; www.flyfishusa.com); Brian Silvey (800-510-1702; www.silveysflyfishing.com); and John Smeraglio (541-395-2565; www.flyfishing deschutes.com). Angling from the boat is not allowed on the Deschutes, and the river is powerful and the bottom slick. A wading staff and cleated wading shoes are strongly recommended.

DESTINATION

37

BROWN TROUT ON
LETORT SPRING RUN

RECOMMENDED BY **Ed Shenk**

Ed Shenk's education as a fly fisherman began on the banks of the Letort more than seventy years ago. "I used to drive to the Bonnybrook area on my bike. It was twelve minutes from home, even closer if I fished in town. Even when I was a tiny boy, my dad would drive me out there. It was thrilling to watch guys catch such beautiful trout. That was what got me into it."

Since it came into the national fly-fishing spotlight more than fifty years ago, the little Letort Spring Run in south-central Pennsylvania is often referenced as one of the pastime's most fabled classrooms. The limestone creek bubbles up south of the town of Carlisle and flows north through meadows and backyards to its confluence with the Conodoguinet River. Fewer than twenty feet wide in many places, rich in aquatic vegetation and riddled with myriad microcurrents bent on disturbing dry-fly drifts, the Letort proved the ideal testing ground for the wiles of Vince Marinaro and Charlie Fox, two anglers who helped shape modern notions of dry-fly fishing. Indeed, the Letort is known as much for the fly-tying innovations it has spawned as for its wild brown trout. Many modern terrestrial patterns (a term coined by Fox) – flies that imitate land-based insects like grasshoppers, crickets, ants, beetles, and the like that fall or are blown into the river – were inspired by the work of Ed Shenk. Ed explained their genesis.

"When I first began fishing the Letort, the trout season closed in July and we didn't give terrestrials too much thought. In fact, my dad and I switched over to bass fishing around July 1. That being said, there was a terrestrial pattern that we fished from Opening Day on, though the term 'terrestrial' was not in the vocabulary. It was a hard-bodied ant, created by a professional tier named Bob MacCafferty. We fished it down and across like a wet fly. We also fished it upstream, on the dead-drift. It was a sinking pat-

OPPOSITE:
Despite its
diminutive size,
Letort Spring
Run supports
some very large
wild browns.

tern. You'd see the fish take. One of the first flies I ever tied was a hard-bodied ant.

"When the season was extended to Labor Day, grasshoppers and crickets became more significant as a food source for the fish. I used to fish number twelve Muddlers dry to imitate hoppers. I was working away from my family a great deal at the time as a mapmaker and had a lot of time to think about new patterns. One day it came to me that hoppers don't have a gold body, so why not make a Muddler with a yellow body. I used angora and a flat turkey wing. My deer-hair head was cylindrical. That was the birth of the Letort Hopper. I blame the Muddler for my design."

Despite its diminutive proportions, the Letort holds some large fish: browns approaching 10 pounds. Stealth is essential in approaching fish, as the Letort's browns are extremely finicky. Anglers must approach in an upstream direction. Crawling on your hands and knees to avoid casting shadows and reflections also helps. "We have lots of guys who hike downstream and put all the fish into hiding," Ed said. "They probably come away thinking that there aren't any fish in the stream." Indeed, despite its notoriety, the Letort is often uncrowded. Many casual fly fishers simply find its fish too discriminating.

Say you're skilled enough to get into proper position, make a pinpoint accurate cast, and hook up with a big Letort brown; how do you go about landing it in such small water? "The main thing is not to bull them," Ed advised and went on to cite two recent examples.

"About five years ago, I landed a twenty-seven-inch fish that we estimated at nine pounds. Just as I got to one pool, I saw a rise twenty-five feet upstream. I was about to cast, then I said, 'Dumbbell, don't cast to the top of the pool before fishing the bottom.' I cast a Letort cricket to the bottom of the pool, just above an underground root system. There was the littlest rise I ever saw, and the fly disappeared. I thought it was a tiny little fish. Then the rod doubled over. I kept just enough pressure on the fish to get him to move upstream. I worked my way over the roots and floating debris and hung on to limbs along the bank to keep my balance. When I got to a level spot, I put pressure on the fish. Like an overweight person, they can be strong for a while, but they wear out quickly. I had four-x tippet on and was able to turn and land it."

The following year, Ed set out with an Orvis 1-ounce, 2-weight rod. He came up to the same root system and could see the back of a big fish in there among the roots. He had to get in the water – which you don't do often on the Letort – to drop the fly in where he thought the fish might be. The fish took the White Minnow and swam over the taproot. "I literally followed him upstream," Ed said, "like I was taking him for a walk. It was a twenty-six-inch brown. When I started to fish again, I noticed a big kink in the leader, in the same spot as where I'd hooked the fish. I never had to give him any line."

The Letort doesn't seem to have the daytime surface activity it's had in the past, and subsurface flies have taken on increasing importance. A lot of Ed's fishing is with a sculpin or White Minnow pattern fished deep, so fish that are hiding under the weeds can see it. Sometimes bouncing the fly along the bottom will work; if fish are moving, a down-and-across presentation will produce.

Ed Shenk has given the angling world many fine patterns over the years, and the Letort has returned him the favor. "I have so many beautiful memories of this river. Not always fish that I caught, but fish that I lost. I've caught a lot of big fish, but I don't go out and get upset if I don't get a big fish. I'm happy to go out and catch a couple fish, regardless of their size. It's great to know I still have it. One of the things that still gives me great pleasure is to pick out a spot where a fish is feeding and get the fly within an inch or two of the rise. And then suddenly you see a fish coming up, up, up, opening its mouth, and then going down with the fly. It still amazes me."

ED SHENK began fishing at age two and caught his first trout by age seven. He has tied flies for sixty-five years; among his many renowned creations are the the Letort Cricket, Flat Wing Letort Hopper, Shenk Cress Bug, and Shenk Sculpin. He served as a fishing instructor at the first Orvis School in Allenberry, Pennsylvania, was the first co-president of the Cumberland Valley Chapter of Trout Unlimited, and has tied flies for President Jimmy Carter. He has published numerous articles in *Sports Afield, Field & Stream, Fly Fisherman, American Angler,* and *American Fly Tier,* among many others. He is the author of *Ed Shenk's Fly Rod Trouting* and is at work on a new book, *Ed Shenk: 65 Years with a Fly Rod.*

IF YOU GO

▶ **Prime Time:** The Letort is open for fishing from mid-April through February. Insect hatches are most consistent in the summer months; that's also when the terrestrials begin popping into the water.

▶ **Getting There:** The south-central Pennsylvania town of Carlisle, which holds a good portion of the Letort, is about thirty miles east of Harrisburg and equidistant from the Philadelphia, Dulles, and BWI airports.

▶ **Accommodations:** There are a variety of motels and hotels in the Carlisle area. For a complete listing, visit www.pacapitalregions.com or call 877-231-ROOM.

▶ **Equipment:** Small waters like the Letort call for smaller rods. A 2- to 4-weight rod in lengths between 6 feet and 8 feet will facilitate the gentle and precise presentations required. A floating line in weight-forward or double taper will work fine. Long, fine leaders are de rigueur on the Letort; 10- to 13-foot leaders tapered to 4x, 5x, or 6x will improve your odds. Carry tippet material in 4x to 6x. During summer terrestrial season, Shenk's Letort Cricket (#10–#18) and Shenk's Letort Hopper (#12–#16) will cover many situations. While hatches are not tremendous on the Letort, you can expect the following at various times of the year: Cress Bugs (#12–#18), Blue-Winged Olives (#18–#24), Midges (#20–#26), Sulphurs (#14–#18), and Tricos (#20–#24). If you can't get anything going on the surface, Sculpins, White Minnows, and Woolly Buggers in #6 to #12 may move the fish. Cold Spring Angler (717-245-2646; www.coldspringangler.com) and Yellow Breeches Outfitters (717-258-6752; www.yellowbreeches.com) can help with flies and also provide guiding services. Ed Shenk (717-243-2679) also guides occasionally on the river.

ATLANTIC SALMON ON THE GRAND CASCAPEDIA

RECOMMENDED BY **Paul Guernsey**

Located on the eastern tip of Quebec, north of New Brunswick, the Gaspé Peninsula is home to ridiculously clear rivers that consistently yield North America's biggest Atlantic salmon. Of the Gaspé's twenty-three major salmon rivers, which include such illustrious waters as the Matapedia, the St. Jean, and the Bonaventure, it is the Cascapedia that offers up the greatest bounty. Multi-sea-winter fish (MSWs) average twenty-four pounds here, and fish over forty pounds are landed each year.

Atlantic salmon were the New World's first great game fish; sportfishing for salmon was first practiced by aristocrats in the late 1700s and has been dubbed the sport of kings. Indeed, Queen Victoria's daughter, Princess Louise, fished the Cascapedia in 1879 and was given rights to the river by the provincial governor. She enjoyed it so much that her husband built her a lodge on the river, Lorne Cottage, which still stands today.

The Cascapedia flows out of the Chic Choc Mountains through rolling hills thickly forested with aspens and pines to the Bay of Chaleur, some eighty-five miles to the south. There are more than a hundred defined pools on the river, divided into discrete and tightly regulated fishing zones. While there are a few areas where a visiting angler can get access on relatively short notice, the better beats are reserved through a dizzyingly complex (at least to outsiders' eyes) lottery system. Bottom line: if you're going to make one trip to this remote and beautiful peninsula and you're not a great planner, work with an outfitter who can provide decent access to the better beats of the river.

Finite salmon waters coupled with a desire to protect these waters from the "riffraff" have made Atlantic salmon fishing a somewhat elitist pursuit. The Cascapedia has such a blue-blood past. At the turn of the century, salmon-fishing rights were leased to wealthy financiers from the south and divided among a group of elite fishing clubs. Many of the

lodges that housed these clubs remain intact, a legacy of a bygone era. In more recent times, the Cascapedia has come back under local control, with beats leased on a lottery system.

Is it merely snob appeal that's gained Atlantic salmon such cult status among anglers? Fortunately, no. The salmon's speckled beauty and its often acrobatic fighting style make it a prized catch. The trick of enticing an Atlantic to take a fly can be one of the sport's great challenges. Like other anadromous fishes that return to the freshwater to spawn, Atlantic salmon feed little (if any) upon entering their home river. They strike a fly for other reasons, as outlined by Hugh Falkus in *Salmon Fishing: A Practical Guide:* feeding habit; aggression; inducement; curiosity; irritation; and playfulness. Other factors that play into an Atlantic's willingness to bite are water temperature (not too cold or too warm), river level (preferably slowly dropping after a big rise), and how many anglers have swung flies before their nose. Many great fishing minds have wrestled with the salmon enigma. One agreed-upon conclusion is that it helps to have luck on your side.

One day in September a few years back, Paul Guernsey was dealt a royal flush. "I have the good fortune to go on a fair number of fishing trips for my work. Some trips go very right, some go very wrong. This one went very right. My voyage to the Cascapedia was my first and only Atlantic salmon trip. The first day on the river I didn't have any hookups, though the water was so clear we could see fish in almost every pool we visited. On the second day, things changed. Using a black-and-orange Woolly Bugger, I hooked and landed a female of forty-six pounds – the biggest salmon taken from the Cascapedia in the year 2000. Before the day was done, I caught another fish of thirty-five pounds. Two fish of a lifetime in one day. I'd like to think I have a special skill for salmon fishing, but the truth is it was dumb luck. My guides, Lee Foran and Perry Coull, did a great job. I was in the right place at the right time."

Guides often rely on sight-fishing. Once fish are spotted, angling techniques are straightforward. Swinging traditional wet-fly patterns down and across is a tried-and-true angling method, though skated flies – and even dry flies fished upstream – will produce. Sometimes it will take a number of different flies and presentations to entice a fish to take ... if they'll take! Imparting a bit of extra action to the fly, either by mending your line downstream or by "pumping" the rod back and forth, seems to help. Fishing is done both from shore and from the twenty-six-foot cedar-strip canoes that are associated with the region. Again, because of the lottery system on the Cascapedia, you'll find little or no

OPPOSITE:
The pools of the Grand Cascapedia regularly surrender North America's largest Atlantic salmon.

DESTINATION

39

competition for good pools. Once you draw a good beat, you're set.

In the course of an extended stay on the Gaspé, it's quite likely that you will draw beats on one of several other rivers in the area – the Bonaventure, the Petite Cascapedia, or the Grande Rivière. This is not a bad thing. These are all first-class salmon rivers with the potential to produce big fish. If Lady Luck isn't with you on the Cascapedia, she might catch up with you on one of the rivers next door.

PAUL GUERNSEY is editor-in-chief of *Fly Rod & Reel* magazine and the author of two novels: *Unhallowed Ground* and *Angel Falls*. He goes on many fishing trips and occasionally is able to make a competent cast with a fly rod. A graduate of the University of Arizona, Paul lives on a farm in Maine with his wife, Maryann, and their two children, Nicholas and Katerina, both of whom were adopted from Russia. When not editing, taking care of kids, or planning bigger and better fishing trips for himself, he devotes his remaining energies to working on another novel.

IF YOU GO

► **Prime Time:** Many of the Cascapedia's biggest fish return from late June to early July. However, the river fishes well from early June through September.

► **Getting There:** The Cascapedia is located in the Bay Region of the Gaspé Peninsula, which is approximately five hundred miles from Montreal and six hundred miles from Boston. Commercial air service is available to the towns of Gaspé and Mont-Joli.

► **Accommodations:** Dunkillie Lodge and Salmon Lodge (418-392-6768; www.gaspe salmon.com) are both situated on the Cascapedia River in the hamlet of Cascapedia St-Jules. Packages include meals, lodging, excellent guides, and permits for river access, and run approximately $3,750 per person (U.S. dollars) for a week's stay, double occupancy. If you choose to go it alone, the nearby seaside towns of Carleton and New Richmond offer a wide range of accommodations.

► **Equipment:** A 9-foot rod in 7- or 8-weight is the preferred weapon. Rods should be outfitted with a floating line. Despite the clear waters, fish are not leader-shy. A 9-foot tapered leader in 0x will work, with 8-, 10-, and 12-pound tippet. Standard Atlantic salmon wet-fly patterns, as well as Bombers, Royal Wulffs, and tube flies all produce.

DESTINATION

39

178

RAINBOW TROUT ON THE
ZHUPANOVA RIVER

RECOMMENDED BY **Guido Rahr**

Kamchatka – a place that may be better known as a minor outpost on the Risk board game than as a destination fishery – is one of the world's last great uninhabited wildernesses. This peninsula adjoining the far eastern reaches of Russia is comparable in size to Japan and bordered by the Pacific Ocean and the Bering and Okhotsk seas. Kamchatka is home to more than twelve hundred rivers (many of which have never been explored), the world's largest population of brown bears (i.e., grizzlies), and some of the healthiest wild salmonid populations in existence. Some rivers hold all five varieties of Pacific salmon, steelhead, white spotted char, Dolly Varden, and rainbow trout.

In recent times, the wild and woolly rivers of Kamchatka have gained some notoriety in fly-fishing circles as steelhead hot spots. The rivers had previously been off limits to Westerners and saw little to no pressure from Russian citizens. Enter the Wild Salmon Center. Since 1994, the group has been guiding scientific expeditions in Kamchatka in collaboration with other conservation groups to ensure the long-term sustainability of the region's fisheries. Working with the newly created Wild Salmon River Expeditions, angling guests can assist in fisheries research by capturing specimens through nonlethal means (e.g., fly fishing) for scale samples and the like. The hope is that such angling tourism can help sustain the rivers *and* the economically troubled people who live nearby. When I asked Wild Salmon Center president Guido Rahr about his favorite fishing experience in Kamchatka, steelhead did not surface, but the giant rainbows of the Zhupanova did.

"The Zhupanova is the most amazing trout stream I've ever encountered," Guido said. "From the size of the trout to the landscape, I don't think a trout stream architect could have designed a better river. And because there are no roads, no dams, and next to

DESTINATION

40

179

no people, the river is exactly as it was five thousand years ago." The Zhupanova is arguably one of the best rainbow trout streams in the world. The fish are exceptionally large, averaging 22 to 28 inches, with fish in the 30-plus-inch range (and eclipsing 15 pounds) caught each year. Visitors can realistically expect to catch the biggest trout of their lives. The fish are not only large but aggressive. Anglers who've made the trek have described floating around a bend to find pods of calmly rising fish, all in the 25-inch class. Unlike most trophy streams, the big 'bows of the Zhupanova see very limited angling pressure; seventy miles of river are shared by a maximum of eighteen anglers on a given week. That means each run is fished on average just two hours a week, leaving the fish undisturbed and ever ready for a tussle. Better yet, the rainbows of the Zhupanova have a delightful proclivity for taking large mouse or vole patterns that are skittered across the water, like a mammal in trouble. The take of a double-digit rainbow on a large surface fly can make you faint! Zhupanova 'bows will also viciously grab streamers fished on sink-tip lines.

If the fishing weren't enough, the Zhupanova is also one of the most scenic rivers in Kamchatka. It flows through a valley of volcanoes that will periodically erupt, snow-capped mountains, huge cottonwoods, birch, aspen, and a potpourri of wildlife that includes caribou, sable, fox, bighorn sheep, and many species of raptors including gyrfalcons and the Steller's sea eagle. The Zhupanova watershed is also home to some very large bears. In the time that expeditions have been led in Kamchatka, there have been many sightings but no incidents.

While Zhupanova anglers are not likely to tire of battling the rainbow trout of a lifetime, other species of fish are also available, including Dolly Varden, kundzha (a sea-going, white-spotted char), and chinook, pink, chum, and coho salmon. The kundzha are a wonderful game fish, averaging 26 to 28 inches, with some specimens exceeding 20 pounds. Summer visitors to the Zhupanova will enjoy especially long fishing days. When anglers come off the river, they're greeted with a cocktail reception that's peppered with traditional Russian toasts. One toast goes something like this:

My great-grandfather said: "I have a desire to buy a house, but I have no opportunity. I have an opportunity to buy a she-goat, but I have no desire." So, let's drink to having correspondence of our wishes and opportunities!

OPPOSITE:
The Zhupanova twists and turns through some of the world's most untrammeled wilderness.

DESTINATION

40

If your wishes involve large rainbow trout, truly wild surroundings, and real adventure, the Zhupanova presents an opportunity you won't be able to resist.

GUIDO RAHR is president of the Portland, Oregon-based Wild Salmon Center, a non-profit organization dedicated to the survival of native salmonids and their ecosystems around the northern Pacific Rim. He has extensive experience working for regional and international conservation organizations, including Conservation International and Oregon Trout, where his work won the President's Fisheries Conservation Award from the American Fisheries Society.

IF YOU GO

▶ **Prime Time:** September to mid-October, as fish bulk up for the winter, is best. May to August also fishes well.

▶ **Getting There:** The staging point for the Zhupanova River is Petropavlovsk, which is a four-and-a-half-hour jet ride from Anchorage. It's served by Magadan Airlines (907-248-2994). From Petropavlovsk, a spectacular helicopter ride showcasing a wild, untamed land brings you to the river. Some people feel the helicopter ride is worth the price of admission.

▶ **Accommodations:** Anglers visiting the Zhupanova have two options. You can choose a float trip, which covers seventy miles of the river, with six permanent tent camps situated along the way. The camps have hot showers, cold drinks, and well-stocked kitchens. Anglers more comfortable with constant surroundings will choose Zendzur Lodge, which overlooks the river and offers private baths. Jet boats hustle you to prime waters. All trips are hosted through the Wild Salmon River Expeditions (800-687-0411; www.steelhead.org). Cost (excluding airfare to Petropavlovsk) is around $4,700 for a week.

▶ **Equipment:** A 9-foot, 6- or 7-weight rod will allow you to cover most wet- and dry-fly fishing situations. A 9-foot, 7- or 8-weight rod is more suited for high-wind situations and for throwing bushy mouse and lemming patterns. Floating and sink-tip lines are used. Leaders should be 7.5 feet long, tapered to 0x, 1x, or 2x. You'll want tippet in 8- to 15-pound test. As for flies, big patterns catch big fish. For the surface, patterns mimicking voles, lemming, or mice (such as Mercer Lemming, Blair Mouse, and Verminator) are effective. Woolly Buggers, Egg-Sucking Leeches, Bunny Leeches, and sculpin patterns (in #2-#4) also produce.

DESTINATION

40

ATLANTIC SALMON ON

THE PONOI RIVER

RECOMMENDED BY **Tarquin Millington-Drake**

Through the latter part of the twentieth century, the notion of catching many Atlantic salmon in a given day's fishing was the stuff of incredible luck – or, more likely, pipe dreams. Then anglers like Tarquin Millington-Drake discovered the Ponoi.

"I first fished the Ponoi in 1992. The fish were extremely free-taking, especially in the spring. Catching tremendous numbers of fish was a new experience to everyone. It made me think of Lord Hume's description of throwing a fly into Scotland's Tweed River from his boat to watch how his fly would swing – and watching fish come up and take the fly in the shadow of the boat. It's like that on the Ponoi so often, it's embarrassing to admit it. The fish are that plentiful, and that eager. It is fun to show the guests who have never seen such things – to watch a fish take the fly right in front of you is fascinating."

Situated just above the Arctic Circle on Russia's westernmost borders, the Ponoi flows west to east, beginning on a tundra plateau in the northern climes of the Kola Peninsula and entering the Barents Sea on the east coast some 250 miles later. The Ponoi is a big river, often averaging more than a hundred yards in width, but its medium flow and shallow depth make it relatively easy to wade and fish. Success in Atlantic salmon fishing is, at least in part, a numbers game, and on most river systems the numbers are not in favor of the angler. This is not the case on the Ponoi. Consider the statistics cited by Tarquin: "Last year, anglers visiting our lodge landed 13,500 fish. I'd say that, on average, each angler caught between thirty and sixty fish – and this figure includes some anglers who have limited or no fly-fishing experience. On our best week in 2003, twenty anglers brought in 1,812 fish; that would be an average of more than ninety fish per angler!"

Not all the fish are MSWs, and fish don't reach the gargantuan size of those found in

183

Quebec or Norway (the Ponoi's best is 30 pounds). Still, the staggering catch rates – even with a number of grilse (immature salmon) in the mix – will leave most anglers elated. It's worth noting that the Ponoi also offers extremely consistent fishing throughout an eighteen-week season; the odds of getting a "bad" week when the fish haven't showed or conditions are unfriendly to angling are low compared to those of most other salmon destinations. Put another way, the worst twelve-year average for a week is seventeen fish per rod.

Except for the rare times when cold or off-color water recommends the use of sink-tips, the Ponoi is a dry-line fishery. Anglers can fish from the boat or from shore, depending on their casting skill and preference. Standard wet flies swung just below the surface produce excellent results. You can also experience explosive takes with skating flies (like greased Muddler Minnows); many who have fished the Ponoi consider it the best skating-fly salmon river in the world. And sometimes it simply doesn't matter what you use. "There was a time recently when I was fishing with a few guides," Tarquin confided, "and decided to have a bit of fun. I had some earplugs from the helicopter ride [from Murmansk], and impaled them on a few hooks. Over the next few minutes, we took five fish on skated earplugs. And that was following twelve fish we had already taken from the exact same spot ... we had three on at the same time twice!

"There's another occasion that stands out in my mind. There's a set of rapids at the bottom of a run we call the Good Water. I had a month guiding on the Good Water and as the water dropped the fish dropped back from the lip of the rapids into them – not your typical holding water. Each day I took my guests there and parked the boat in the heart of the rapids. Waves were all around us, and I instructed my anglers to start casting. They thought I was crazy. Moments later, they were into the first of many fish, including one of twenty-five pounds."

Salmon anglers seeking quietude will appreciate the Ponoi experience. There are no roads, and twenty guests share fifty miles of water with the occasional reindeer and falcons. Be sure to bring bug repellent; from early July through early August, large numbers of mosquitoes are present on the tundra.

Isolation does not mean an absence of jubilation on the Ponoi. "We've assembled guides from a great number of nationalities who mix well with our Russian staff," Tarquin said. "Guests genuinely enjoy the staff and atmosphere of the camp. There's a tremendous feel-good factor. At dinner, staff and guests are not separated. We celebrate

OPPOSITE:
The Ponoi
is considered
one of the
most prolific
Atlantic salmon
fisheries in
the world.

DESTINATION

41

together, and the toasts are frequent and heartfelt." Catch statistics are not the only validation of a great salmon river, yet the results anglers have seen on the Ponoi seem to promise a place for this river in Atlantic salmon fishing lore. "On the Ponoi, our best days are not behind us," Tarquin said. "We're still looking forward. It's fun to be part of creating history."

TARQUIN MILLINGTON-DRAKE first fished the Ponoi in 1992 and enjoyed many seasons as a representative for Frontiers International Travel before taking over as manager and president of the Ponoi River Company in 1999. Born in Australia but living in the UK, Tarquin has fished for Atlantic salmon in Canada as well as extensively in Scotland, Iceland, Russia, and Norway. He has also fished in Mexico, the Bahamas, Venezuela, Argentina, Chile, Christmas Island, Seychelles, New Zealand, Canada, Alaska, Belize, Mongolia, England, and Costa Rica.

IF YOU GO

► **Prime Time:** Catch rates on the Ponoi are highest in early June, though the river fishes well through September.

► **Getting There:** Murmansk, Russia, is the staging point for Ponoi journeys, and Murmansk is generally reached from Helsinki, Finland. Both are served by Finnair. A noisy but reliable helicopter (included in your fare) transports you from Murmansk across the tundra for two hours until you reach the Ryabaga Camp on the Ponoi.

► **Accommodations:** The Ryabaga Camp (www.ponoirivercompany.com) is a comfortable tent camp on the river with excellent meals, a friendly staff, and unexpected amenities like an on-staff massage therapist. A week on the Ponoi will range from roughly $4,500 to $9,500, depending on when you visit.

► **Equipment:** Spey rods in the 9- to 10-weight class are the most commonly used weapon on the Ponoi. While fast-sinking tips are useful at the beginning and the end of the season, floating lines will work for the remaining months. Have at least 150 yards of backing on your reel. A 9-foot leader tapered to 12- or 15-pound test will suffice. Proven patterns include Ally's Shrimp, Thunder and Lightning, Mickey Finn, Yellow Ally, and Willie Gunn, tied on tubes or double hooks in sizes #2 to #6. Bombers and Muddler Minnows tied on single #4s and #2s are popular skating patterns.

ATLANTIC SALMON ON
THE RIVERS DEE AND TAY

RECOMMENDED BY **Árni Baldursson**

Where does a renowned Icelandic Atlantic salmon guide and entrepreneur choose to go for a fishing holiday? If that salmon aficionado is Árni Baldursson and it's springtime, it's the River Dee; if it's the fall, it's the River Tay. Both in Scotland. "I've been fortunate enough to fish all over the world, but there's something special about Scotland," Árni said. "The people are very nice, the whisky is wonderful, and there's such a wonderful salmon fishing tradition. It's simply such a joy just to be there. Salmon fishing is different in Scotland than in Iceland. You have to be picky about the beat. If you're on the right beat on the right river at the right time, it can work well. You have to choose wisely. When I'm in Scotland, I have a lower expectation to catch fish – you need fewer fish to be happy there. Being on the banks of these famous rivers that people have fished for so many generations is enough."

While both are catalogued among Scotland's premier salmon fisheries (along with the Spey and the Tweed), the Dee and the Tay are vastly different systems. The Dee is perhaps Scotland's most scenic salmon river. It begins high in the Cairngorm Mountains and flows swiftly for ninety miles through the Aberdeenshire countryside to the North Sea at Aberdeen. (The region is home to the royal residence at Balmoral, and hence is often called Royal Deeside.) The Dee is a spring fishery, with fish caught as early as February and salmon reaching the upper river by late May. It seldom goes off-color and clears quickly if it does. The river is divided into three sections; Árni's favorite beat is Lower Crathes on the lower river, downstream from Banchory. While the Dee suffered diminishing fish returns in the early 1990s, elimination of commercial netting operations near the mouth and catch-and-release policies have shown good results. In 2001 (the most recent statistics available at publication time), 3,400 salmon were landed on the Dee.

"The Dee is gin clear – the clearest of all Scottish salmon rivers," Árni said. "You can fish floating lines and smaller flies – it's a delight! It's dream fly water. Every pool seems to have been made for fly fishing. I have done pretty well on the Dee over the years. In my best week of fishing, I landed twenty-two fish." Where the Dee can seem intimate, the River Tay is quite big through most of its seventy-odd-mile course to the Firth of Tay at Dundee. Flowing out of Loch Tay in Highland Perthshire, the Tay starts large at more than 125 feet in width. By the time it's joined by the River Tummel midway through its eastward journey, the Tay is about 250 feet across, with strong currents and deep pools. It runs with a slightly peatish tint. The Tay boasts both a spring (May/June) and fall (September/October) run of salmon and is the UK's most consistent producer of larger fish, in the 30-pound class. In 1922, a 64-pound fish was taken from the Glendelvine beat on the Middle Tay by a young lass named Georgina Ballantine; it still stands as the UK record.

Arni's favorite beat on the Tay is Lower Redgorton on the lower river. "For me, the attraction of the Tay is the excitement of having the opportunity to catch a big trophy," Árni said. "The fish are very powerful, but you have to work very hard for each and every fish. It requires very long casts. You use all of your skills. You must be prepared for sink-tip lines and very big flies during higher water conditions. However, if the water is low, you can fish very light with floating lines and even a riffling hatch. I caught a twenty-five-pound fish that way."

As the caddies of Saint Andrews help connect visiting duffers to the heritage of time-tested links, the ghillies of Scotland's salmon rivers pass on far more than angling advice; they are an essential part of a fishing holiday. Many beats are passed from father to son, generation after generation. A day with one of these river stewards places you in the long continuum of the Scottish salmon angling tradition. But it's not all gravitas. Many ghillies have a tremendous sense of fun, as Árni recalls. "This is the story of when I almost dropped down dead. For ten or twelve years, I've always gone to Scotland on my own, leaving my wife back in Iceland. A few years back, my ghillie – a wonderful fellow named Robert Harper – and the folks at Banchory Lodge conspired to set me up. As I was finishing up lunch one day in the lodge, someone ran up to the table and said, 'Árni, there's a twenty-five-pound fish in the top pool. You've got to go out.' Of course, I grabbed my rod and ran outside. As soon as I was set up on the pool, some people from the lodge came down and scolded me – 'Árni, why are you poaching this water?' Somewhat confused and frustrated, I returned to the lodge, thinking a bit of whisky was in order. The lodge was rather dark and quiet. I went to where the decanter was kept and began pouring myself a glass. Then I heard my wife's voice – 'Árni, you're drinking too much!' I think that everyone in the valley knew my wife was coming and was in on the joke."

ÁRNI BALDURSSON is among Iceland's foremost fishing outfitters. His Angling Club Lax-a (www.lax-a.is) manages a number of Atlantic Salmon rivers in Iceland, including beats on the East and West Ranga. In the off season, Árni leads hunters in Iceland and Greenland and often visits the Caribbean, Central America, and South America to pursue salt- and freshwater species with his fly rod.

IF YOU GO

► **Prime Time:** The River Dee fishes best March to May. For general information on leasing beats, visit www.dsfia.org/fishing_beat.html; for the Lower Crathes beat, contact Stuart Young at +44 1330 86 02 23. The River Tay fishes well in May/June and September/October. For general information on leasing beats, visit www.fishingnet. com/river_ tay.htm. Pricing for beats varies greatly, and can range from £100 per day to much more. Many beats come with a resident ghillie as part of the deal.

► **Getting There:** Kincardineshire on the River Dee is roughly 125 miles north of Edinburgh; Stanley on the River Tay is roughly sixty miles north of Edinburgh.

► **Accommodations:** For the River Dee, Banchory Lodge (+44 1330 82 26 25; www. banchorylodge.co.uk) in Kincardineshire is Árni's preferred dwelling. Rooms are from £70. It's right on the river and often accommodates for anglers. For the River Tay, Árni likes Ballathie House Hotel (+44 1250 88 32 68; www.ballathiehousehotel.com) near Stanley, another angler-oriented abode. Rooms are from £75.

► **Equipment:** Spey rods of 14- or 15-feet in 9- or 10-weight are the tools of the trade on Scottish rivers, where two-handed rods were born. On the Dee, anglers will generally find good results with a floating line; popular patterns include Stoats Tail and Hairy Mary tube flies. On the Tay, sinking lines are often necessary during high- and cold-water conditions with large flies like a Willie Gunn or Black and Yellow tube fly. When the water drops, sink-tips and even floating lines with patterns like Ally's Shrimp, Tummel Shrimp, Stoats Tail, or Munro Killer can be effective.

DESTINATION

42

BONEFISH ON
ST. FRANÇOIS LAGOON

RECOMMENDED BY **Joe Codd**

Joe Codd succinctly summed up the bonefishing to be experienced at St. François Lagoon in the Seychelles: "It may mess you up for the rest of your life." The "messing up" comes from the Seychelles' absurdly large numbers of bonefish (locally called "banane"), fish that average 4 to 6 pounds and are not terribly prissy. "If you can cast forty feet, you have a good chance to catch twenty fish in a day," Joe explained. "Your casting doesn't even have to be very precise, because the fish aren't that picky. They are generous fish."

The Seychelles rest in the Indian Ocean, a thousand miles off the east coast of Africa and six hundred miles north of Madagascar ... which is to say, not particularly close to anywhere. This, of course, explains why the islands went undiscovered for so long (sportfishing didn't open up here until the late 1990s). From their discovery in 1502, the Seychelles bounced back and forth between French and English control before gaining independence in 1976. Historically, for economic sustenance the islands' inhabitants relied on cotton cultivation, whaling, coconut plantations, and the export of guano. Since gaining independence, the government has set aside nearly half of the total area as nature reserve or parks, and tourism has flourished.

St. François Lagoon is situated near Alphonse Island, roughly 180 miles south of Mahé, the Seychelles capital. Visitors stay at Alphonse Island Resort, which is a half-hour run from the lagoon. Once they reach St. François, anglers are transported to the flats in skiffs. The flats are firm, providing easy wading; most anglers will stalk bonefish on foot. With nearly twenty-five square miles of flats and a very finite number of anglers, solitude is a good bet. Fish tend to travel in small groups, giving anglers the opportunity to target individual fish. Action is fastest when the tide is on the move. In addition to large num-

OPPOSITE:
Anglers working the flats of the Seychelles may encounter more bonefish than they imagined possible.

DESTINATION

43

191

bers of fish and a large average size, St. François hosts fish into the teens (several International Game Fish Association world records have already come from the region). Noted angler and photographer Brian O'Keefe described Seychelles fishing as "Florida-sized bonefish, Christmas Island numbers."

When the tide is out at St. François Lagoon, anglers willing to hike a bit can witness a wonderful spectacle, as Joe described: "There's a reef at the edge of the lagoon that's about a mile out, roughly a forty-five-minute hike when the water is low. If you go out there and stand on the edge of the flats you can watch the fish stage up by the reef to come in on the incoming tide. The fish come in by the thousands, in schools ranging from ten to two hundred. It's like they're surfing."

There's an unexpected fallout to the Seychelles' bounteous bonefish gifts: boredom. "When you're fishing the Seychelles and hooking twenty or thirty bonefish in a day, it can get a bit old," Joe said. "On my first trip, we started with seven-weights and ended with nine-weights, so we could bring the fish in quicker. At one point, I started cutting my leader back and switching flies, without adding any additional tippet, just to see if there was something they wouldn't take." The good news is that there are a number of other fun and interesting species to fish for. There are giant trevally, bluefin trevally, pompano (the Indian Ocean's version of permit), grouper, triggerfish, and emperors. There's also some great blue-water fishing. Joe fished along the reefs from a skiff for giant trevally, which are fantastic sport. He even fished GTs in the surf with poppers and streamers. Joe's group hooked GTs up to 40 pounds and landed one around 35 pounds. Many of the fish there get much larger.

An ancient species of fish – the milkfish (known locally as "pati pati")– is beginning to emerge as the hottest sport fish available around the Seychelles … and perhaps any-where. "I've had several clients who have fished for milkfish," Joe related. "Most of these guys have caught big tarpon and bonefish. They come back and tell me, 'If you would've told me it would take me an hour and a half to land a twenty-pound fish of *any* species, I would've hung up the phone. After breaking two rods out there, I'm a believer.'" Milkfish are tricky to put the fly in front of, as their routines are unpredictable. They're vegetarian, which poses fly challenges that the guides at St. François are just beginning to figure out. "If you get one to take," Joe added, "they go absolutely beserk. They jump like a tarpon, and rip line off at twice the speed of a big bone. If you hook up, you need to jump in a skiff and chase them. You simply can't stop them on a nine-weight. The guides try to steer them toward the sand and land them there. They've been breaking too many rods trying to land them in the boat."

While milkfish hold great promise, in the near term it is bonefish that will draw visitors to the Seychelles. And if one has any questions about the profligate numbers of bonefish in St. François Lagoon, consider the following tale that Joe related: "It rained most nights while I was there, but cleared each morning. One night, we sat around discussing what a ridiculous notion it was to blind-cast to bonefish. The next day, we woke up and it was still raining. We decided to go out anyway. We had an hour left on the tides, so we decided to head out toward a channel that was about a half mile away to fish for giant trevally. As an afterthought, we picked up our bonefish rods to dink around on the way out to the channel, as our guides were carrying our ten-weights. We began pitching flies into the flats, which were murky from the rain. Suffice it to say, we never made it to the channel. We caught nonstop bonefish for two straight hours, even though it was squalling and we couldn't see a single fish until it was on the beach. They were all good-sized fish, averaging six pounds. Between the three of us, we must have landed sixty fish. Over lunch, all we could say was 'Remember what we were talking about last night?'"

JOE CODD is the saltwater program manager for Frontiers International Travel. Before joining Frontiers, Joe worked for L. L. Bean, Inc., for fifteen years as a technical support person for sporting goods, primarily hunting and fishing, and as lead instructor for Bean's fly-fishing schools in Freeport, Maine. Joe has had the opportunity to fish some of the most beautiful places in the world – French Polynesia, Christmas Island, Hawaii, the Yucatán, Belize, Costa Rica, Panama, Guatemala, the Seychelles, Nicaragua, the Bahamas ... and even in the United States! Representing Frontiers in the 2003 "One-Fly" tournament at Jackson Hole, Wyoming, Joe took individual top honors for the event.

IF YOU GO

▶ **Prime Time:** The fishing season runs from the second week in September to the second week in May. Traditionally, you can expect windier conditions during May and September. For good background information, visit www.seychelles-flyfishing.com.

▶ **Getting There:** Anglers traveling from America can transit through either Paris or London. Seychelles International Airport in Victoria is accessed from various European

DESTINATION

43

gateways via the services of Air Seychelles, British Airways, and K L M / Kenya Airways.

► **Accommodations:** Anglers fishing St. François Lagoon generally stay at Alphonse Island Resort (www.alphonse-resort.com), a fine hotel with thirty air-conditioned, beach-front chalets, tennis courts, and a pool. World-class scuba diving is also available. Rates are $4,790 per person for a seven-night/six-day stay based on double occupancy. Rates include accommodations, shared guide and skiff, all meals, and round-trip airfare between Mahé and Alphonse Island.

► **Equipment:** You'll need a variety of tackle to fully embrace the Seychelles experience: For bonefish and smaller trevally: 9-foot 8-weight rod with floating and sinking line and at least 150 yards of backing; 3 to 5-foot monofilament leaders with tippets from 8- to 16-pound test. Flies should include Crazy Charlies, Gotcha, Minipuffs, Bonefish Specials, and Clouser Minnows, (#2–#8). Small poppers will work for trevally. For giant trevally: 9-foot 10-weight rod with floating and fast sinking lines and 250 yards of backing. Flies should include sardine, anchovy, squid, and mackerel patterns, plus Lefty's Deceivers, Gurglers, and poppers in #1/0 to #3/0. For milkfish: 9-foot 11- or 12-weight rod with a floating line and 300 yards of backing. Your guides will set you up with the proper leader and flies, based on their research.

BROWN TROUT AROUND
PERALEJOS DE LAS TRUCHAS

RECOMMENDED BY **James Prosek**

A few years back, James Prosek was on a crusade across the earth's 41st parallel in search of pure-strain trout. At one point his quest took him to Spain. A quixotic endeavor? Not if you have an equally zealous friend who knows where to go. "Johannes Schoffmann and I are both obsessed with native trout," James said. "Johannes is a baker in Austria. Ever since we met in 1995, we've taken a trip each summer looking for wild fish. Spain was somewhere we wanted to go. There's good food, good wine, and we could speak the language, at least a little. Spain is remarkably wild, at least compared to France and Germany. It can be a bit desolate, but many places seem frozen in a simpler time."

Spain does not leap to mind for most Americans as a fly-fishing destination, though literature majors may recall Hemingway's adventures there on the Rio Irati near Burguete, as channeled through his alter ego, Jake Barnes, in *The Sun Also Rises:*

> While I had him on, several trout had jumped at the falls. As soon as I baited up and dropped in again I hooked another and brought him in the same way. In a little while I had six. They were all about the same size. I laid them out, side by side, all their heads pointing the same way, and looked at them. They were beautifully colored and firm and hard from the cold water.

(We must forgive Jake for the expediency of using worms; you may recall that Jake's accomplice, Bill Gorton, caught larger fish downstream using flies.)

Spain has a rich fly-fishing history, documented as early as 1539 in a work called *The Little Treatise on Fishing,* and offers fly fishers some wonderful prospects. There are twenty-six rivers that support fishable runs of Atlantic salmon; Spain is the southernmost outpost of Atlantics in Europe. There are also countless trout streams that flow throughout the country, with especially good concentrations of rivers in the Basque region (the locale of Jake Barnes's fishing exploits), the Pyrenees, and Andalucia. Many hold native brown trout as well as rainbows that have been introduced. "Most people don't realize that the dictator Francisco Franco was a fanatical fisherman," James observed. "He closed off entire rivers to public access so he could fish them himself. Some of the streams he reserved for his own use are still the best fishing." The number of rivers that hold pure-strain fish, however, is quite finite. "In the winter months, Johannes had been researching the state of native trout in Spain," James explained. "In the process, he got his hands on a paper from a graduate student named Garcia at the University of Barcelona. Garcia and his colleagues had identified what was believed to be the last pure-strain brown trout in Spain. The home of this trout was a small, unmapped tributary of the Tajo River in the province of Guadalajara."

The tributary is called Rio de la Hoz Seca, or River of the Dry Gorge, and is located near a town called Peralejos de las Truchas. Rio de la Hoz Seca is separated from the Tajo by a waterfall, making crossbreeding between mixed-strain Tajo browns and pure-strain Hoz Seca fish impossible. "*Truchas* is Spanish for trout, and we figured that any town with 'trout' in its name was a good omen," James said. The roads leading to Peralejos went from bad to worse, but eventually James and Johannes reached the village. "Peralejos de las Truchas is made of stone, and has maybe two hundred people," James continued. "It seemed a somewhat forgotten place, though I think that at certain times of the year, it's a bit of a fly-fishing destination for Spaniards visiting the Tajo, which is a fine river in its own right. Peralejos is not exactly Livingston, Montana, but there were people who seemed to be there for the fishing." The seekers' past experience had shown that the local bar could be the best source for angling information – and, for that matter, any other information – so that was where they headed. A friendly barmaid offered cold beer, tapas, and good directions to the river. The next day, the two adventurers set out to find their quarry.

"The trip to Rio de la Hoz Seca from Peralejos was just long enough to give us a sense that we'd gone somewhere," James recalled. "There were no signs, but the directions were perfect. Rio de la Hoz Seca rivals any river I've seen in terms of beauty. The greens of the water and vegetation are a wonderful contrast to the earth tones of the surrounding canyon." And just as important to the crusade, the creek was filled with large trout.

Working the creek's undercut banks, it didn't take James long to come up with a fine 17-inch specimen of the Atlantic drainage brown trout he and Johannes had been seeking. "The fish was a brilliant yellow, with prominent vertical bands," James continued. "It resembled a Mediterranean brown, though the Tajo flows to the Atlantic. Johannes surmised that the fish's ancestors might have crossed over from the Mediterranean drainage. It was a trout that was completely new to us, and we were thrilled." After photographing the trout in a glass tank they carried for that purpose, James and Johannes released the fish and celebrated with a bottle of wine, in true Hemingway fashion.

"Knowing that the fish had not been contaminated, that it swam in its pure, virgin state, is an incredible realization," James mused. "You know the fish was meant to be there. They just have this look about them."

JAMES PROSEK has been called the "Audubon of the fishing world" by no less an authority than the *New York Times*. He published his first book, *Trout: An Illustrated History*, at the tender age of nineteen, while a junior at Yale University. James has gone on to show himself an equally competent author, penning *Joe and Me: An Education in Fishing and Friendship, The Complete Angler, Early Love and Brook Trout, Fly Fishing the 41st*, and most recently, *Trout of the World*. His curiosity and passion for native trout have taken him around the world; he's currently at work on a book about eels.

IF YOU GO

► **Prime Time:** The trout season in Spain is open from March 26 to July 30, though some regions are open for catch-and-release fishing through the end of September.
► **Getting There:** Peralejos de las Truchas is about 125 miles east of Madrid. The roads are narrow and not particularly well marked; to reach Rio de la Hoz Seca, you'll have to take a series of four-wheel tracks. James noted that it's a place for "adventurous spirits."
► **Accommodations:** There are a couple of places to stay in Peralejos de las Truchas: Tajo del (+34 949 83 70 34) and Los Quiñones (+34 949 83 70 50). Rooms with a bath are about $30. The bars in town serve tasty, inexpensive food in the Spanish tapas tradition.
► **Equipment:** A 9-foot 4- or 5-weight rod with floating line will suffice for Rio de la Hoz Seca and the Tajo River. The bartender at the Bar Jube in town ties beautiful flies and is an excellent source for angling information.

DESTINATION

44

BROWN AND RAINBOW TROUT

ON THE GREEN RIVER

RECOMMENDED BY **Bret Carlson**

In 1962, anglers visiting the Green River near Dutch John, Utah, could anticipate casting to squawfish, chubs, and suckers. Not exactly the stuff of fishing vacations. With the completion of the Flaming Gorge Dam in 1963, all of that changed. The perennially off-color Green was transformed into a virtual spring creek, flowing crystal clear at ideal trout temperatures. Brown trout were planted in the river at this time, and have since thrived. The browns, combined with introduced populations of rainbows and cutthroat, make this one of the most prolific trout rivers in the United States. In the seven-mile "red canyon" section immediately below the dam, fish populations can approximate fourteen thousand trout per mile. Thanks to an incredibly fecund biomass especially rich in scuds (a form of freshwater shrimp), the fish grow large fast, adding a couple of inches per month in the spring and early summer. Many trout eclipse 20 inches, and fish exceeding 24 inches are commonly seen, though not commonly caught.

OPPOSITE: Crystal-clear water, thousands of big fish, and a prolific cicada emergence make for memorable times on the Green.

Bret Carlson has been fishing the Green since he was eight when his uncle, noted guide Monty Howard, began teaching him to fly fish. "The vast numbers of fish and their size – the fish average at around 16 inches – make the Green a standout." Bret said. "My favorite aspect of the Green is the water clarity, especially in the sections of the river above Red Creek Rapids. You're able to get a wonderful perspective on fish behavior. If you're fishing a nymph nine feet down in a pool, you can see the fish take the fly – even before the indicator moves. Or you can watch the fish move several feet from their feeding spot to chase a big dry fly and eat it."

For fly fishers, the thirty miles of the Green below the dam is like three rivers. Section A is enclosed by steep, red rock canyons and, due to its large fish populations, sees the most angling pressure. As you continue downriver, the canyon opens up and fish num-

DESTINATION

45

bers decrease. However, the average size of the fish *increases*. On the last fourteen miles of the river, large browns – most over 17 inches – predominate, though it's estimated that fewer than a thousand fish per mile populate this section. This is true Wild-West country, the former haunt of Butch Cassidy, the Sundance Kid, and the Wild Bunch. Be sure to look up from the river now and again to take in the scenery.

If you're looking for a chance to put large numbers of fish on the boards, you'll probably want to float section A – though understand that you won't be alone (at peak season, hundreds of anglers will float section A on a given day). If you're looking for more solitude and the chance for trophy browns, sections B or C might be more to your liking. Fishing from a drift boat allows anglers to reach the greatest number of likely lies – seam lines, cliff sides, grassy banks, and subsurface structures. If walking and wading are more to your liking, a well-maintained path follows the river for the first ten miles down from the dam.

While nymphing and stripping streamers will yield good results on the Green, most visiting anglers focus on the river's several notable insect hatches, which bring the wary, bigger trout to the surface. In early spring, one of the West's most prolific Blue-Winged Olive hatches comes off, with the smallish mayflies blanketing the water. It seems as though you can cross the river on the snouts of feeding fish. On warmer winter days, midge fishing provides consistent surface activity.

It's the Green's terrestrials, however, that provide a singular opportunity to take large fish on large flies. Hoppers, Mormon crickets, aquatic wasps, and a variety of ants and beetles all provide large food fodder – it seems that one man's pestilence is another man's pleasure! If there's one terrestrial that typifies the Green River experience, it's the cicada. Cicada is the largest member of the suborder *Homoptera*, which include leafhoppers, treehoppers, and aphids. They're not a common menu item on most trout streams. As nymphs, they live underground and feed on the roots of trees and shrubs. When they leave their burrows in late May, they climb the trunks of trees, their skins split open, and mature cicadas emerge. Their clicking or buzzing noise, a sound that speaks to the arrival of summer in many locales, is a siren song to trout and anglers alike.

If you've worn through eyeglass prescriptions trying to thread a #20 Black Gnat to your 7x tippet, let alone follow it in the current, cicada patterns are a joy. Some are tied on #2 hooks and are as big as your finger. On the flat water, they ride like the *Queen Elizabeth II*, and they remain very visible even in riffles. Needless to say, the trout like them too. "If Blue-Winged Olives are crackers on the trout plate," Bret quipped, "cicada are cheeseburgers!" Casting straight downstream with a continued long drift is a great way to trigger explosive strikes from fish waiting in ambush. Fishing right to the bank also produces well, as the Green's browns lie in absurdly shallow water – presumably waiting for the next Big Mac to fall. When the fish do come up, don't set the hook right away. It takes the fish a moment to get its mouth around the big fly and setting too soon will pull the fly away. During cicada time, big flies plus big fish equal big fun.

BRET CARLSON is part owner of Spinner Fall Guide Service, based in Dutch John, Utah, and guides on the Green and Provo rivers as well as other local streams. He has also guided in the Quebec/Labrador region on the Champdoré system. A graduate of the University of Utah, Bret tries to take a break from guiding the Green in September so he can chase steelhead throughout the Northwest and British Columbia.

IF YOU GO

▶ **Prime Time:** Cicadas generally emerge in good numbers in mid to late May. Activity continues in earnest through June. The good news is that, due to the vast number of cicadas that the trout eat during this period, they continue to key in on large artificials throughout the summer. The Blue-Winged Olive hatches begin in mid-March and continue through mid-May.

▶ **Getting There:** The area of the Green of interest to fly fishers is located in the northeast corner of Utah, near the Wyoming and Colorado borders. It's a four-hour drive from Salt Lake City and five and a half hours from Denver.

▶ **Accommodations:** In the Dutch John area, there are several lodges, including Flaming Gorge Lodge (801-889-3773), Red Canyon Lodge (435-889-3759), and Spring Creek Ranch (307-305-3005).

▶ **Equipment:** A 9-foot 5- or 6-weight rod outfitted with floating line will work for most situations; 4x leaders will suffice, with tippet ranging from 2x to 6x. Green River aficionados rely on a number of patterns to mimic the cicadas. Favorites include the McFly-style Cicada, the Noble Chernobyl, and the Calf Wing Cicada, in sizes from #2 to #12. Guide services include Spinner Fall Guide Services (877-811-FISH; www.spinnerfall. com) and Western Rivers Flyfisher (801-521-6424; www.wrflyfisher.com).

BROWN TROUT ON THE

BATTENKILL RIVER

RECOMMENDED BY **David D. Perkins**

It's not clear whether or not "help wanted" postings for Orvis's corporate headquarters near Manchester, Vermont, mention the building's close proximity to the Battenkill. If they do, it might cut both ways – the company would certainly recruit some passionate anglers for their ranks, though absenteeism credited to maladies like the "Hendrickson flu" might escalate.

    "The ties between Orvis and the Battenkill are very strong," Dave Perkins said. "For many, the two are synonymous. I don't think the company would have been created if it wasn't for the river. The Orvis family ran hotels in the area in the 1850s, and they catered to outdoors people and anglers. They began building fly rods for their guests' use."

    The Battenkill has its headwaters in southwestern Vermont, near the town of Manchester. It flows for twenty-five miles in Vermont through idyllic countryside, and for another twenty-four miles in New York before entering the Hudson River. In its Green Mountain State reaches, the Battenkill is populated by wild brook and brown trout. There are good numbers of browns in the 14- to 16-inch range, and some fish at 20-plus inches. Battenkill browns are notoriously wily, made all the more so by the incessant false casting of the many anglers who make the pilgrimage to fish them.

    "As long as I can remember, the Battenkill was considered a challenging stream," Dave said. "It's always had enough pressure to make the fish very wary, even before fly fishing had entered the mainstream. Hatches typically occur just before the last light of the day fades. It's a period of about forty-five minutes, until it's pitch dark. If you don't have a pretty good idea of what fly the fish are focusing on, you're in trouble, as you'll waste most of the good forty-five minutes of fishing time trying to figure things out. People who fish the Battenkill a lot – like a lot of the employees at Orvis – do well.

OPPOSITE:
The wary brown trout of the Battenkill see a lot of flies. Landing a larger brown here is quite an accomplishment.

DESTINATION

46

They can exploit the previous evening's lost opportunities."

Several factors combine to make the Battenkill a tricky fishery. The river's pace is generally slow, and there's little structure in the middle of the river. This sends the fish toward the banks where rocks, willows, alder, and overhanging bushes provide good cover. From here, the fish have the leisure to carefully critique each offering that flows past. Flies that get caught up in microcurrents and display the tiniest bit of drag don't stand a chance.

Within a short distance of Manchester, the Battenkill takes on three different characters. First, it's a few smallish streams, the east and west branches, very tight, with lots of overhanging trees. Just south, it's slow, flat water, with a silt bottom. The silt produces different hatches and requires a different style of fishing. From the town of Arlington down, it's more of a freestone bottom, predominately riffle water. There's more bug activity on this stretch.

"I feel that a fly-fishing experience is closely connected to a mood," Dave said. "On the Battenkill, it's easy to match your fishing to your mood. When I want to catch a number of fish and see more bug activity, I like the Arlington section. There are springs that come in, which create nice brook-trout sections. When I want to go after bigger fish, I love the upper flat water. You kind of know from experience where the big fish might be. You might work on a certain fish all summer, always wondering if he'll be in his spot and willing to take."

The memory of Dave's first big Battenkill brown still burns strong. "It was early evening. The sun had set, and the moon was casting a glare on the water at the perfect angle to silhouette my fly. I could make out a big fish sipping bugs under tree branches, also in the path of the moonbeam. I cast over and the fish took my number eighteen fly. It was an eighteen-inch brown. The fish, the path of my fly, and the moonlight were all in alignment. Otherwise, I wouldn't have been able to see anything. It was perfect."

Small moments like this define the Battenkill. Fishing writer John Merwin perfectly captures the quiet grace of this river in his wonderful book *The Battenkill: An Intimate Portrait of a Great Trout River – Its History, People, and Fishing Possibilities*:

You can catch more and bigger trout in Montana, pop a few beers at the Grizzly Bar, and listen to a honky-tonk jukebox down by the Madison. It's a loose, fun, uninhibited kind of fishing. The Battenkill is more like Bach; with green hills, covered bridges, and white-clapboarded villages forming the gently repeating steps of a sweetly insistent fugue in which rising trout play an occasional part.

DAVID D. PERKINS is executive vice president of the Orvis Company. He currently oversees its wholesale business, retail business, and the fly-fishing and wing-shooting schools. Dave also directs the Orvis Travel Service and its offering of international fly-fishing, wing-shooting, and adventure travel destinations. An avid fly fisherman and wing shooter, Dave sits on the board of the Ruffed Grouse Society and is past president of the Southern Vermont chapter of Trout Unlimited.

IF YOU GO

▶ **Prime Time:** The Battenkill is open from the second Saturday in April to the last Sunday in October. Mid-May to mid-June sees the greatest proliferation of hatches, but autumn angling offers the bonus of Vermont foliage. If water levels are adequate, the river can fish decently through the summer.

▶ **Getting There:** The town of Manchester is a good staging area for fishing the Battenkill. Manchester is about two hundred miles north of New York City, and 125 miles northwest of Boston.

▶ **Accommodations:** Greater Manchester is awash in quaint bed and breakfasts. A few possibilities include the Battenkill Inn (800-441-1628; www.battenkillinn.com); the 1811 House (800-432-1811; www.1811house.com); and Ira Allen House (888-733-8666; www.iraallenhouse.com).

▶ **Equipment:** A lighter rod in the 3- to 5-weight class, outfitted with floating line, will work. The Battenkill's browns demand delicate presentations, calling for 9-foot to 12-foot leaders in 5x and 6x, with tippet material from 1- to 5-pound test. To see what's hatching, visit the flagship Orvis store (802-362-3622) or the Brookside Angler (802-362-3538). Guide services are available from Blue Ridge Outfitters (802-747-4878; www.blueridge outfitter.net) and Peter Basta (802-867-4103; www.vtflyfishingguide.com). Before the evening hatch comes off, visit the American Museum of Fly Fishing in nearby Brookside (802-362-3300; www.amff.com).

DESTINATION

46

SMALLMOUTH BASS ON THE
SHENANDOAH RIVER

RECOMMENDED BY **Harry Murray**

Some people will fish for smallmouth bass with a fly rod if they can't get to a trout stream. Harry Murray will fish for smallmouth in his beloved Shenandoah River *in addition to* chasing trout in nearby mountain streams.

"I like to say that the smallmouth bass is the gentleman of the warm-water species," Harry explained. "If you do things properly, he will respond. I have excellent trout fishing close by in the mountains, but I find smallmouth fishing a welcome addition to trout fishing. In fact, smallmouth feed a tremendous amount like trout. The tactics one might use for browns and rainbows in the Rockies will take bronzebacks here." On many levels, smallmouth bass (*Micropterus dolomieu*) bear a greater resemblance to trout than to their jug-bellied cousins, the largemouth bass. Bronzebacks prefer cool, clean water, appreciate quicker river currents, and are scrappy fighters, with far more endurance than largemouth bass. Smallmouth are catholic feeders, preying on sculpin, minnows, crayfish, hellgrammites, frogs, and even mayflies.

The Shenandoah River is considered one of the nation's premier smallmouth fisheries, with both great numbers of fish and stable populations of larger fish. The Shenandoah and its two major tributaries, the North Fork and the South Fork, offer more than 150 miles of fishable water, flowing in the shadow of the Blue Ridge and Allegheny mountains. The river reaches its terminus when it joins the Potomac at Harper's Ferry, West Virginia. The Shenandoah's fish are not native to the river; they're thought to have originated in Wheeling Creek, West Virginia, and were introduced to the Potomac in the 1850s by railroad employees with a penchant for angling.

"The Shenandoah is a very productive river," Harry said. "Fish average eight to ten inches, but we're getting more large fish now than I ever remember. We had one in 2002 that topped twenty-four inches! Bass are distributed throughout the system – they're not just limited to the riffle areas. There really are no bad stretches." Taking a boat down the river allows you to cover the most water. Sometimes anglers will wade pools and runs; other times you'll fish from the boat. A great thing about bass fishing on the Shenandoah is that you can use a variety of methods to take fish. Streamers – say a Murray's Madtom or a Clouser – cast across and stripped back on the swing below riffles or up against the bank will produce well. Upstream nymphing, just like you might do on a western trout river, also generates good results. Casting popping bugs into shady lies against the shore is great fun, as you see all the action. The greatest challenge using poppers is getting bigger fish to come up to the surface. A lot of the big fish are taken earlier in the season. As the season goes on, the fish become more cautious.

"Over the years, I've gotten to know the Shenandoah very well," Harry said. "I know the areas that have historically given me big fish. As these fish are very territorial, I know that if I caught a good fish at a given spot once, there will probably be a fish – maybe the same fish – there again. There are certain bass that I feel I've gotten to know. It gets very personal. Some of the largest bass I've caught take a surface fly the same way a big brown trout does. They just come up and suck the popping bug under, with no sound at all."

Whereas the rivers of Kamchatka or Patagonia can be a bit difficult to access on short notice, the Shenandoah is within easy reach of the D.C. beltway. There are many points where anglers can access the river to launch a drift boat or canoe, and the river is easy to navigate for do-it-yourselfers. (There are also several guides who ply the river.) And for newcomers to fly fishing, the smallmouth of the Shenandoah can be a great confidence booster. Whether you're casting poppers or stripping streamers, there's little question that an angler will catch fish; the uncertainty lies in how many and how big. With good conditions, an experienced angler can expect as many as sixty fish in a day's float.

A bass float on the Shenandoah offers an opportunity to contemplate the rich Civil War legacy of the valley. A critical agricultural region for Confederate forces and a relatively short march from Washington, the Shenandoah Valley was the site of many battles, including Stonewall Jackson's famous campaign of 1862, when he beat back Union regiments despite their far greater resources. With the exception of a few power lines, bridges, and modern farm implements, the land itself is little changed from the days of pitched warfare.

HARRY MURRAY was trained as a pharmacist and is owner of Murray's Fly Shop in Edinburg, Virginia. He is the author of many articles and five books, including *Fly Fishing for Smallmouth Bass, Virginia Blue Ribbon Streams,* and *Trout Fishing in Shenandoah National Park;* he's also produced several videos, such as *Fly Fishing for Smallmouth Bass* and *Mastering Mountain Trout Streams.* An avid photographer, as well as a professional fly tier and designer and rod builder, Harry has taught fly fishing at Lord Fairfax College for twenty-five years.

IF YOU GO

▶ **Prime Time:** June is the peak smallmouth season on the Shenandoah, as spring flows have dropped but the water has not warmed too much. The fish are getting in a spawning mood at this time, and are aggressive. The river fishes well from early May through mid-October.

▶ **Getting There:** Edinburg is a good base for fishing the Shenandoah, and it's not quite a hundred miles from Washington, D.C. Beware – with proximity comes weekend canoeing crowds. If possible, get to the river during the week.

▶ **Accommodations:** There are many bed and breakfasts in the Shenandoah Valley; see a comprehensive list at www.bbhsv.org.

▶ **Equipment:** A 9-foot, 6- or 7-weight rod is perfect for tossing some of the larger flies you'll need on the Shenandoah. Floating line will work for 90 percent of the fishing; a fast sink-tip might come in handy in the early spring and fall. Nine-foot 2x leaders are good for floating line, a 5-foot 2x leader for sinking line. Your fly box should include Shenandoah Sliders in orange and yellow (#6), Shenandoah Blue Poppers (#6), Murray's Hellgrammites (#4–#8), Strymphs (#4–#8), and Shenk's White Minnows (#4–#6). Murray's Fly Shop in Edinburg (540-984-4212; www.murraysflyshop.com) can set you up with everything you need. Harry Murray and his associates also offer guide services.

BROWN AND RAINBOW TROUT
ON THE FIREHOLE RIVER

RECOMMENDED BY **Dan Callaghan**

The poet Robert Frost once contemplated whether the world would end in fire or ice. He didn't entertain the possibility that fire and ice might somehow combine to create what some consider to be the strangest – and many consider to be the finest – trout stream on earth: the Firehole.

The Firehole gurgles alongside geysers and bubbling fumaroles, forever cloaked in steam and a faintly sulphurous odor that's a constant reminder of the unique geothermal properties that are both the river's bounty and its bane ... at least as far as fly fishers are concerned. The injections of hot water into the river's snowmelt-cold headwaters result in a mineral-rich broth that fosters abundant insect life, which sustains healthy populations of wild brown, rainbow, and cutthroat trout. (Incidentally, only the cutthroat are indigenous to the Firehole; rainbows and browns were introduced in the late 1800s.) The same thermal waters, hot enough to poach a careless fish, make the Firehole uninhabitable in many stretches in the warmer summer months; at these times, trout move into feeder creeks like Nez Perce, Sentinel, and Fairy Creek. Geothermal hijinks aside, the Firehole's beauty and abundant wildlife are enough of an attraction to woo many anglers, including Dan Callaghan. "I have so many wonderful memories of this little river," Dan said, "fishing with dear friends – the Phantom (James Nelson), Ernie Schwiebert, and Jack Hemingway. Fishing on the Firehole isn't easy. But it's just so glorious to be there."

The Firehole flows from tiny Madison Lake as a wee mountain creek. By the time it has meandered for a few miles, passing Old Faithful and gaining the flow of the Little Firehole near Biscuit Basin, it's a premium trout stream. Over the next dozen miles, anglers can dodge bison, sidestep mud pots, and experience some of the most challeng-

209

ing – and satisfying – dry-fly fishing they could hope for. The smooth-water sections of the Firehole that flow through the meadows below Biscuit Basin have many of the complex subcurrents of a spring creek, making good drifts a precious commodity. The fact that one section of the water column might be scores of degrees warmer than the one to the right or the left only further complicates matters. "If you want to fish with a dry fly, you've got to wait for something to happen," Dan said. "You can nymph with good results, but most of the time I'll just sit and wait for a hatch." Those who fish the Firehole often know better than to charge onto the river in front of anglers who seem to be watching clouds pass by. Those sky-gazing folks are waiting for a hatch to come off; give them space and they'll return the favor.

The meadow sections of the Firehole have enough weed cover, holes, and undercut banks to provide ample hiding spots for the fish. When a hatch comes off, the larger fish will position themselves near such cover to warily sip on the variety of stoneflies, mayflies, and caddis that the river produces. Through much of its length the Firehole is bordered by the Grand Loop Road, hence the fish see not a few offerings. Long leaders, light tippets, and a delicate upstream approach will help your odds, as will smaller flies. Here, as much as on any spring creek, you'll do well to match the hatch as precisely as possible. "I remember one occasion when a hatch of flavlinea were coming off," Dan said. "I was fishing with Ernie Schwiebert, and we didn't have quite the right pattern. We went up to the car, and Ernie somehow tied a few flies up using his thumb as a vise. They worked!" Many of the Firehole's residents are in the 12- to 14-inch class; trout to 20 inches and above are present, though not often encountered by any but the most skilled and patient anglers. Amidst such spectacular surroundings, size *does not* matter.

Great rivers like the Firehole evoke great memories. Two of Dan's involve his dearly departed friend the Phantom, so named because he would often appear at his friends' side at rivers around the West unannounced. "The animal life and wildflowers of the Firehole make it a wonderful place for a photographer," Dan said. "One of my favorite photos shows the Phantom casting against a whole bank of wildflowers, with a bull bison reclining just above the flowers." When the Phantom passed away, his friends returned him to his favorite trout stream. "We had a little ceremony on the Firehole with Craig and Jackie Mathews, Bud Lilly, and Dr. Pat Daley. We scattered the Phantom's ashes in the river. I'm not sure how the park service would feel about that, but I know it helps the Phantom's soul be at rest."

OPPOSITE: The Firehole's unique geothermal properties create a one-of-a-kind fishery.

DESTINATION

48

DAN CALLAGHAN is an attorney and photographer. In addition to conducting a successful law practice, Dan has shot the photographs for *Thyme & the River*, *Thyme & the River Too*, *Fishing Yellowstone Waters*, *The Waters of Yellowstone with Rod and Fly*, and *A River Seen Right*. Dan is the creator of the Green Butt Skunk, one of the world's most popular and reliable steelhead flies. He was a founder and served on the boards of the North Umpqua Foundation and the Steamboaters. He was the Federation of Fly Fishers' general counsel for fifteen years and served five years as a Oregon Department of Fish and Wildlife Commissioner. In 1986, Dan received Oregon Trout's Wild Trout Award; in 2003, he received the Federation of Fly Fishers' Charles Brooks Memorial Life Award.

IF YOU GO

▶ **Prime Time:** The fall is probably the best time to fish the Firehole, as water temperatures have moderated. The early half of June can also be good. The river is open from the Saturday before Memorial Day through early November.

▶ **Getting There:** The closest available commercial flights go into West Yellowstone, which is served by SkyWest (www.skywest.com), and Bozeman, which is served by Alaska Airlines (www.alaskaair.com), Delta (www.delta.com), and Northwest (www.nwa.com). Bozeman is two hours from West Yellowstone. Visitors can also fly into Salt Lake City and drive the six hours to the park.

▶ **Accommodations:** West Yellowstone, Montana (just outside the boundary of the park), is rife with moderately priced hotels. The West Yellowstone Chamber of Commerce (406-646-7701; www.westyellowstonechamber.com/lodging.htm) has a comprehensive list. For information about accommodations and camping in the park, contact Yellowstone National Park Lodges (307-344-7311; www.travelyellowstone.com).

▶ **Equipment:** A 9-foot 4- or 5-weight rod outfitted with floating line will work on the Firehole. Bring 9-foot leaders tapered to 5x or 6x, and tippet material from 2- to 5-pound test. The many fly shops around West Yellowstone, including Blue Ribbon Flies (406-646-7642; www.blueribbonflies.com) and Bud Lilly's Trout Shop (406-646-7801; www.budlillys.com), can help you determine what patterns are working best.

BROWN AND RAINBOW TROUT
ON THE MADISON RIVER

RECOMMENDED BY **Craig Mathews**

Some visitors to Yellowstone National Park will linger at the campground just below the confluence of the Gibbon and Firehole rivers, and perhaps even make a few casts into the river that's born there. The water is very warm and rich in minerals, thanks to the Firehole's geothermal activity, and the river bottom undulates with plant life. Few fish are caught here and tourists continue on to the West Yellowstone Park exit, perhaps thinking that it's too bad there are no fish in that pretty river that skirts the road. Little do they know that they've been following one of the most fabled trout streams in the world!

For fourteen miles inside of Yellowstone National Park – and for another 120 northward miles to its terminus at the Missouri River – the Madison River offers myriad fly-fishing experiences, all of them great. There are fast-water riffles, deep holes, smooth runs, and everything in between, offering dry-fly aficionados, nymphers, and streamer fishers wondrous opportunities to take wild brown trout that average 17 inches and wild rainbows that average 14 inches. The trouting challenges presented on the Madison combined with the backdrop its incomparable environs provide have made an outing on this great river a rite of passage for generations of anglers, including the best and brightest of America's fly-fishing visionaries.

If there's a contemporary angler whose legacy is connected with the Madison, it's Craig Mathews, proprietor of Blue Ribbon Flies in West Yellowstone. "The Madison is like two world-class trout streams – one in the park, one outside of the park," Craig said. "In the park, you can match wits with large browns while bull elk bugle and square off and bison feed within a stone's throw. On the lower river below Quake Lake, anglers can enjoy thirty- and forty-fish days, either wading or floating. The fishing is just that good." Thanks to the likes of Charles Brooks, Lee Wulff, A. J. McClane, and others, the stretch-

es of the Madison inside the park read like a who's who of famous fishing holes. Every angler planning a trip to Yellowstone – even if it's not specifically a *fishing* trip – has contemplated an afternoon at Nine Mile Hole, Grasshopper Bank, Cable Car Run, or Barn Hole Numbers One, Two, and Three. (There are a number of holes in the "Behind the Barns" area. The story goes that only the first three were named because turn-of-the-century anglers never proceeded beyond Barn Hole Number Three. By that time they had reached their limit of twenty-five trout.)

OPPOSITE:
Fishing the
Madison in
Yellowstone,
one is as likely
to encounter
bison and
elk as wild
browns and
rainbows.

The rich mineral content of the Madison inside the park makes for complex bug life. Pale Morning Duns, Blue-Winged Olives, Tricos, Green Drakes, and a variety of caddis all make summer appearances on the river. As alluded to above, grasshopper patterns can also be devastatingly effective when fished against grassy banks – at least until the first few frosts. In the deeper, quicker runs, heavy salmonfly nymphs fished near the bottom are a reliable producer. While the Madison in the park has generated bookshelves of classic fishing literature, the Madison outside of the park – especially from Lyon Bridge to Ennis, Montana – logs the most fishing hours. In his *Madison River Journal,* author John Holt reckons that "more fly fishers have taken their first trout on this stretch of river than any other in the world." The annual salmonfly hatch, which comes off in late June and early July, brings out the masses ... not surprising when one considers the visceral thrill of casting large Sofa Pillows to willing fish. A variety of caddis make an appearance on the river here, and terrestrials will also sometimes work. With the abundance of *Pteronarcys californica* throughout the system, stonefly nymphs are always a good bet if nothing is happening on top. "Something that many people don't realize is that many sections of the Madison are open through February, and provide excellent dry-fly action," Craig added. "The river is at its lowest point at this time, and very clear. Midges hatch consistently and the trout key on them. I'd say that you'll see more rising fish on the Madison in the winter than any time of the year, especially below McAtee Bridge."

Beyond its wonderful trout and illustrious anglers, the Madison holds another tale, a story of conservation and redemption. In the early 1990s, a plague of whirling disease afflicted the Madison and many fish were lost. Thanks in part to information campaigns targeting the angling community, the rapid spread of whirling disease has been checked, and fish populations are steadily edging toward pre–whirling disease numbers. Like so many western rivers, the Madison has been subject to water draw-downs and shoreline degradation brought on by agricultural and cattle interests. Conservation and sporting groups have worked diligently to preserve riparian habitat by consulting with ranchers and buying up land whenever possible. The $3 Bridge Project is one example of how concerned anglers can take control of their destiny. In this case, a rancher needed to sell his land, which adjoined a mile and a half of river frontage. Craig and other members of the $3 Bridge coalition raised the money necessary to purchase the land in question, making it forever protected and open to fishing.

"Everybody that I pass on the river thanks me," Craig recalled. "I'll always remember one occasion in particular. A six-year-old girl came up to me in the shop and gave me fifty cents. She said, 'Listen Mr. Mathews, I stole this from my dad because he loves the river. I think I can get fifty cents more.' Even the developers who work in the area pitched in to help. We have the plaque from the Montana Fish, Wildlife, and Parks commemorating the $3 Bridge Project near the door of our shop."

CRAIG MATHEWS served as police chief of West Yellowstone, Montana, before opening Blue Ribbon Flies in 1980. He's gone on to become a great expert on western fly fishing. Craig is the author of five books: *Fly Patterns of Yellowstone*, *Fishing Yellowstone Hatches*, *The Yellowstone Fly Fishing Guide*, *Western Fly Fishing Strategies*, and *Fly Fishing the Madison River*. Committed to protecting and preserving wild trout habitat, Craig and the folks at Blue Ribbon Flies have received numerous awards for their conservation work from groups like the Nature Conservancy and Federation of Fly Fishers. He recently cofounded the 1% for the Planet Club; member businesses donate 1 percent of gross sales to support conservation projects.

IF YOU GO

▶ **Prime Time:** Though hatches change, the Madison can fish very well throughout the year. Many anglers converge on the lower sections of the river in late June for the salmonfly hatch. Likewise, fly fishers seeking large migrating brown trout frequent the lower sections of the park water (focusing on the Barn Holes) in early fall.

▶ **Getting There:** The closest available commercial flights go into West Yellowstone, which is served by SkyWest (www.skywest.com) and Bozeman, which is served by Alaska Airlines (www.alaskaair.com), Delta (www.delta.com), and Northwest (www.nwa.com). Bozeman is two hours from West Yellowstone and closer to Ennis, a main staging area for the lower river. Visitors can also fly into Salt Lake City and drive the six hours to West Yellowstone.

▶ **Accommodations:** West Yellowstone, Montana (just outside the boundary of the park), has many moderately priced hotels. The West Yellowstone Chamber of Commerce (406-646-7701; www.westyellowstonechamber.com/lodging.htm) has a comprehensive list. The Ennis Chamber of Commerce (406-682-4388; www.ennischamber.com) also lists accommodations.

▶ **Equipment:** A 9-foot 5- or 6-weight rod outfitted with floating line will serve you well on the Madison. With so many blue-ribbon rivers nearby, there are probably more fly shops and fly-fishing guides per capita in the greater Madison River region than anywhere else in the world. A couple of good bets are Blue Ribbon Flies in West Yellowstone (406-646-7642; www.blueribbonflies.com) and the Madison River Fishing Company (800-227-7127; www.mrfc.com) in Ennis. While you should consult with local fly shops about current hatches, a few Madison standbys include Kaufmann's Stonefly Nymphs in black, brown, and olive (#4–#8); Stimulators and Sofa Pillows for the salmonfly hatch (#6–#12); grasshopper patterns (#6–#12) in the summer; and black Woolly Buggers (#6–#10) for big browns. The Grizzly Bar and Grill (406-682-7118) near the Madison in Cameron, Montana, is a favorite watering hole for anglers.

TIGER FISH ON THE ZAMBEZI RIVER

RECOMMENDED BY **Larry Dahlberg**

The Zambezi River runs some sixteen hundred miles across southern Africa as it surges toward its terminus at the Indian Ocean in Mozambique. At times a raging torrent punctuated by dramatic waterfalls, at others a mellow mile-wide flow, the Zambezi is a river with many faces. To Larry Dahlberg, stretches of the Zambezi are quite reminiscent of the St. Croix River in Minnesota, where Larry began guiding fishermen at the tender age of eleven. Reminiscent, except there were no crocodiles or hippos in the St. Croix.

Suffice it to say, the close company of some very large animals, and many fish with very large teeth, sets the Zambezi fishing experience somewhat apart from your average trout fishing trip. According to Larry, tiger fish (*Hydrocynus vittatus*) or the "striped river dog," have "the fuselage of a bonefish, the tail of a tarpon, the paint job of a striped bass, teeth like a bull shark, and a compound hinged jaw that works like a turbo-powered paper shredder. They may be the most capable and impressive freshwater predator on earth."

Larry first fished the Zambezi in the mid-eighties, when he floated hundreds of miles of the river in several exploratory ventures. Parts of the river were fairly populated, especially upstream of Victoria Falls. Below the falls it was much less populated. There were times when Larry's party could see no people but heard the drums from the interior that seemed to signal an awareness of their presence. At that time, the world-record tiger fish was 6 pounds. Conventional wisdom was that they couldn't be caught on artificial lures, only on bait. The preferred bait was tiger-fish flesh, which says something about these creatures' predatory nature. Ox flesh was used to catch the first tiger fish.

"The water in the Zambezi is very warm, in the nineties in some places," Larry said. "This makes the fish's metabolism very fast. We were fishing with lures at first, and had to snap-retrieve very quickly to get the fish to strike. We caught thirty to forty fish and had

OPPOSITE:
Outfitted
with ferocious
choppers, tiger
fish are aptly
named.

a sense of what we needed to do to get them. I figured it was time to try the fly rod. Some of the male fish we caught were milking sperm, so we knew it must be spawning time. We knew from our research that the tigers liked to spawn near a floodplain, so we went downstream from Chiawa Lodge [within Lower Zambezi National Park] to find it. Once we reached the floodplain, I rigged up with a fast-sinking line, tied on a Dahlberg Diver, and cast toward shore. On the third cast, I thought I'd hooked a crocodile. The fish catapulted out of the water – it was in the high teens, three times the size of the current world record!" With that fish, a new adventure fishery was born.

Fly fishing for tiger fish is not a complex business. Any habitat that provides cover for an ambushing predator – boulders, submerged trees, ledges – supports tiger fish. Smaller fish in the 2- to 3-pound range are often found closer to shore. Larger fish frequent steep drop-offs. Tigers in the double digits are considered good catches; fish up to 20 pounds have been caught. While fish will occasionally take surface poppers, a deep approach is more productive, as the Zambezi's water clarity in Lower Zambezi National Park is limited. Tiger fish are built to prey on creatures up to two-thirds of their size, but a large fly is not necessary. A flashy fly – anything with a lot of flashabou – will do the job if retrieved quickly. Hooking a tiger when it strikes is the greatest challenge, as its mouth is very tough. Keep hooks sharp and strike hard.

Once hooked, a tiger fish is good for some spectacular leaps and frenzied runs. "They jump and jump and jump," Larry said. "They don't have terrific fighting longevity. That's probably because of the warm water." When you get a tiger fish to the boat, exercise care. Those choppers will penalize sloppy release techniques. Focused tiger-fish anglers can anticipate steady action on the Zambezi. Five to ten fish a day in the 8- to 10-pound class is common, with a few larger fish in the mix. You can also expect twenty-plus fish in the 5- to 7-pound range, and as many smaller tiger fish as you'd care to catch.

One of the constants of fishing the Zambezi is the omnipresence of hippos. While often docile, they have potential for great violence and are reputed to take more human lives than any other African mammal. Given a decent berth in the river, the hippos will keep to themselves. However, anglers will do well to be off the river by dark, as the hippos become more active and disagreeable as the sun goes down. The hippos display an odd behavior called wheeze-honking that can be exploited by the savvy angler – the savvy angler with a strong stomach. "Wheeze-honking seems to be a territorial response," Larry explained. "The hippo makes a braying sound like an outboard with the prop half out of the water. While braying, the hippo pees, poops, and twirls its tail at the same time. Smaller creatures in the river like to feed on the nutrients in the hippo poop. And tiger fish like to eat the little creatures. If we come upon a hippo wheeze-honking, we fish the current a bit below the hippos."

However you fish the Zambezi, you'll find yourself in the midst of jungle wonderland teeming with wildlife. You may drift past a herd of elephants on the bank or encounter a pride of lions over a fresh kill. "I've been on a number of safaris in game preserves," Larry said. "It's not as organic an experience as fishing on the Zambezi. The Lower Zambezi National Park around Chiawa has not been turned into a theme park. It's real. I think fishing here is a better game experience than you'll get at many game parks."

LARRY DAHLBERG is the host of ESPN's *The Hunt for Big Fish;* in filming the show, Larry has landed five dozen fish larger than existing world records. He has been described by John Randolph of *Fly Fisherman* as the most successful "big fish" fly fisherman ever. Larry has won numerous OWAA awards for his work and is the only fishing television producer to be nominated for two ACE awards. In 1990 Larry received the prestigious Henshall Award from the Federation of Fly Fishers for his promotion of warmwater fly fishing. He was inducted into the Freshwater Fishing Hall of Fame in 1996 and received the International Game Fish Association Conservation Award in 1999.

IF YOU GO

► **Prime Time:** September through November is the peak season for hunting tiger fish in Lower Zambezi National Park.

► **Getting There:** It is not a short trip to the Zambezi. Most travelers fly into Lusaka, Zambia, which is served by British Airways and South African Airways. American travelers generally reach Lusaka from London or Paris. From Lusaka, it's a forty-minute charter flight into the Jeki Airstrip, and a few more hours by Land Rover to Chiawa Camp. Even the most skilled Internet travel planners will want to use a booking agent to coordinate this adventure.

► **Accommodations:** Chiawa Camp (www.chiawa.com) is located on the banks of the Zambezi in the Lower Zambezi National Park and can accommodate up to six anglers at a time; this is the setting Larry Dahlberg described. Guests stay in well-appointed tents, complete with bathrooms and hot and cold running water. The Afro-Euro cuisine is first rate. The lodge was voted one of Conde Nast's top ten safari camps. When you're not on the river, you can participate in game safaris. Cost is approximately $550 per day per person, based on double occupancy. Cindy Garrison's Safari Anglers (www.safari-anglers.com) and Zambelozi Island Lodge (www.flyfishingafrica.net) also offer tiger-fishing adventures.

► **Equipment:** Bring a 9-foot rod in either 8- or 9-weight and several high-density sinking lines as well as a weight-forward floating line, and at least 100 yards of backing. Short, heavy tippets (20-pound test is sufficient) are the order of the day. Be sure to use a wire leader, as the tiger fish's teeth will make quick work of even the heaviest nylon. Almost any baitfish pattern will work, as long as it has a bit of flashabou. Popular patterns include Dahlberg Divers, Clousers, and Lefty's Deceivers in red, black, orange, white, chartreuse, and yellow, tied on #2/0 hooks.

Excerpt on page 195 is from *The Sun Also Rises* by Ernest Hemingway,
copyright 1926 by Charles Scribner's Sons. Copyright renewed 1954 by Ernest Hemingway.
Reprinted with permission of Scribner, an imprint of Simon & Schuster Adult Publishing Group.

Excerpt on pages 204-205 is from *The Battenkill* by John Merwin, copyright © 1993 John Merwin.
Reprinted with permission of The Lyons Press, an imprint of Globe Pequot Publishing.

Edited by Jennifer Lang · Production by Kim Tyner
The text of this book was set in Scala.

Printed and bound in Thailand by Imago

Book Design by Paul G. Wagner